Touch and Go

Original Edition – 1993
Enhanced Edition – March, 2018

…to enlighten, to inspire, to educate,
…to astound, to delight, to amuse,
…to imbue with a sense of wonder….

Dr. Hilarion M. Henares Jr., known as **Larry Henares,** is a graduate of Ateneo de Manila, University of the Philippines, and the Massachusetts Institute of Technology, an engineer, economist, educator, big businessman, writer, civic leader, public servant, and hobbyist (guns, books, amateur radio and electronics).

He is a writer known for his essays on economics, history, art and culture, a front page columnist in the pre-martial law Manila Times and the most widely read column in the Philippines, according to all surveys, the daily "Make my Day" in the Philippine Daily Inquirer, after the EDSA revolt.

ooooo

Tatay Jobo Elizes, Self-Publisher

This book is published under permission of

DR. HILARION (Larry) M. HENARES, JR.

ISBN – 13: 978 - 1986797627
and ISBN – 10: 1986797627

ooooo

About the book "Touch and Go":

Just like the previous 13th book, this 14th book of the Make My Day Series "Touch and Go" concerns itself with Personalities and Perspectives.

The first part includes an essay on Senator Raul Manglapus, the quintessential Atenean and his rivalry with Senator Pelaez; historian Carlos Quirino, his encounter with President Manuel Quezon in the nude, and his bid to be recognized as a National Artist; and Mayor Alfredo Lim and his bid for the Presidency. You will laugh at his description of the most miserly family in the Philippines; whose toilets are used five times before being flushed to save on water, whose members do not give Christmas gifts to each other, and fight to the death to retrieve pennies dropped on the pavement. And of course, Jaime Zobel who sued Henares for P240 million, the biggest claim for damages in Philippine jurisprudence.

And hilarious accounts of Larry's experiences with the Customs and Claude Wilson who got caught bringing in dutiable goods like electronic appliances, cigarettes and liquor; Ramon Diaz, whom he called Raymond THE Ass; Jojo Binay who should be glad he is not as tall and conspicuous as Victor Lim; Nikki Coseteng and Col. Maganto who beheads students; General Singlaub who plots Vietnam type operations in the Philippines; the homosexuals of Dasmariñas Village; and the Arab terrorist of San Lorenzo Village.

. The second part, Perspectives, features a 17-part series on How To Serve The Americans by the Council of Trent, the Makati Business Club, and the Four Horsemen of the ConComm. It also features a hilarious account of the "apotropaic rites" of the Press Gridiron Night; and a commencement speech to end all commencement speeches, telling of the three levels of genius, and giving a picture of the Philippines 100 years hence. Lastly a hilarious piece on sexual harassment and the mating game; and a serious one on the Holy Wars that plague the world.

Henares is a unique writer who can make you cry, and laugh, and get mad at the same time.

oooooo

BOOK 14 - TOUCH AND GO
TABLE OF CONTENTS

ooooo

PERSONALITES

ooooo

CHAPTER 1. Raul Manglapus, Blue Eagle the King

Part 1. Raul Manglapus, the quintessential Atenean
     There is such thing as a Great UPian, because as a concept UP does not exist. There are only the UP fraternities, and they are eternally at war with each other. There are no Great Opus Dei, either, for they are all under the Spaniards, and they have no other purpose in life but to accumulate wealth and power, disdain the poor, and serve the foreigners.

     There are no Great LaSallites because there is no such thing as a LaSallite. There are only the La Salle Mestizos, the coño boys subsidized by the Sorianos and Zobels; the La Salle Chinese who own the Philippines; and the poor LaSalle Filipinos who are left to fend for themselves; and the three are not even talking to each other. They don't even understand each other, for one speaks Spanish, another Fokien and the other Taglish.   There are two who might have been great

Filipino LaSallites, Lorenzo Tañada and Jose W. Diokno, but they have never been honored as such. The only ones so honored by the Christian Brothers are the ones who pursue wealth, like the del Rosario brothers, Concepcion twins, Danding Cojuangco and someone called Chris Concepcion before he ran off with somebody else's money.

The greatest Ateneans are Jose Rizal and Claro M. Recto, men of genius and Renaissance spirit. But they were repudiated by their foreign Jesuit mentors because they were Filipino patriots. Other great Ateneans were Horacio de la Costa and Leon Ma. Guerrero. But Horace became more of a Jesuit than a real Atenean, and Leonie became a patriot prematurely, hitting the Americans when the Filipino people were still under the spell of Americans. On the other hand, Emmanuelle Pelaez remained a pro-American even after we became independent.

Only Raul Manglapus can truly be called a Great Atenean. He was pro-American when the American Jesuits still controlled Ateneo, and became a patriot only when Filipino Jesuits took over. The Jesuits and students of Ateneo never faltered in their admiration and support for Raul Manglapus, for in their eyes and in the eyes of many, he was the quintessential Atenean. Every other Atenean was measured by the standards set by Raul Manglapus. His Arrneoow accent and facility with a dozen dialects and languages was legendary.

Raul Manglapus was my school-boy hero. As a boy, I was there when he when he delivered his speech "Land of Bondage, Land of the Free," lost the oratorical contest, and was publicly commended by President Quezon as the one who should have won. I was there when he delivered his famous speech "His Excellency, Labor," with which he won the First National Oratorical Contest. I was there when he composed "Blue Eagle The King," to cheer our teams to victory. I was there when he graduated *summa cum laude.*

I bore witness to his incarceration and torture by the Japanese, his dramatic escape from Los Baños POW camp, his exploits as a guerrilla, and eventually, after Liberation as the only Filipino to attend the surrender ceremony of the Japanese on the Battleship Maine in Tokyo Bay.

My wife Cecilia and I spent our first visit to Disneyland

in the company of Raul and Pacing Manglapus. I followed him wherever he led us, into Magsaysay's Rah Rah Boys, supporting him as our youngest Foreign Affairs Secretary under Magsaysay. When Magsaysay died, I joined him and Manahan in the latter's failed bid for the presidency. I was with him in the Progressive Party, and in the Grand Alliance in his quixotic bid for political recognition.   (to be continued)

Part 2. Raul's rivalry with Manny Pelaez
There was a time when Raul Manglapus and Emmanuelle Pelaez, both prominent Ateneans, strode into the political arena together, sometimes in partnership, sometimes in rivalry. Manny Pelaez was not a wartime hero as Raul Manglapus was, but during the Occupation, he spent hours at home singing "God Bless America." During the war, Raul Manglapus fought in Bataan, was incarcerated and tortured by the Japanese, made a dramatic escape from the Los Baños POW camp, and participated in the Liberation of Manila.

After the war Manny Pelaez, a bar topnotcher, became a special prosecutor in the People's Court. He was with Magsaysay and the Nacionalista Party along with the Rah Rah boys of Raul Manglapus. Manglapus composed the famous campaign song "Mambo Magsaysay," and tutored Magsaysay in oratory, specially the famous Moises Padilla speech that ushered Magsaysay into the Presidency. He served Maysaysay as Secretary of Foreign Affairs. After Magsaysay died, Manny and Raul ran for the senate under the Grand Alliance (PPP Progressives + disgusted Liberals and Nacionalistas), and lost.

In 1961 as an LP, Manny Pelaez became Vice President under Diosdado Macapagal, in whose cabinet I served. Manglapus topped the senate race, and distinguished himself with the sponsorship of the Land Reform Act. Manny wanted to be president, but with Macapagal eyeing a second term, both he and Marcos left the LP to join the NP. Marcos won the nomination, and Pelaez drifted back to the PPP with Manglapus as presidential candidate.

"When I come back from Cairo, I'll campaign for you," Pelaez told Manglapus in 1965. Pelaez never showed up, instead he ran with the LP (and Macapagal), and on TV asked the voters not to waste their votes on Manglapus.

In 1969, Pelaez was back with the NP, campaigning for Marcos whom he once called a "most dangerous man." In 1972, martial law was declared, and three senators were immediately ordered arrested -- Ninoy who was imprisoned seven years, Pepe Diokno in prison for two years, and Raul Manglapus who escaped and was in exile for 13 years. Pelaez became Minister of State for Foreign Affairs, and defended Marcos from the attacks of Manglapus in Hawaii as late as 1980, and stayed with Marcos till he was ambushed by persons unknown, after which he laid low, while the rest of us were fighting the February Revolution. I never saw him in a public rally.

Raul Manglapus was to be Ambassador to the USA, but somehow Manny Pelaez ingratiated himself with Cory and got the appointment instead. Manglapus was elected into the Senate. Eventually Cory appointed Raul Manglapus as Secretary of Foreign Affairs, and as such he negotiated with asshole Americans on the US Bases, and did his best to promote, protect and defend Philippine interest in the face of his boss President Cory Aquino's determination to accommodate the Americans. A majority of twelve Senators led by Jovito Salonga, Wigberto "Bobby" Tañada and Erap Estrada opposed and rejected the Bases Treaty.

Raul Manglapus accepted the position of Chairman of the Philippine National Oil Co., in the administration of President Fidel V. Ramos, and spent many a time playing with his Executive Band with First Lady Ming Ramos as pianist, and once with US President Bill Clinton as saxophonist when he was here on a visit.

During Erap's term, Raul Manglapus retired, contracted throat cancer, and passed away peacefully.

August 30 and 31, 1999 on DWBR-fm; August 4 and 6, 1999, Philippine Post

ooooo

CHAPTER 3. Carlos Quirino as an Artist

Part 1. Deserving awardee

"Malacañang shouldn't give in to lobbyists for National Artists Award," screamed the headlines on page E2 of the Inquirer dated Sunday, October 12.

The article written by an Alex Gallago of Paco, Manila, accused an unnamed child of an artist of unwarranted lobbying. Denden Quirino, daughter of biographer Carlos Quirino, called me up in tears because she felt alluded to. But I consoled her by saying that I was the suspected lobbyist. And I resent those assholes in the National Commission of Culture and Arts who think the awards are exclusively theirs to distribute among themselves, many of whom do not deserve the honor. On September 5,1997, I wrote the following memo to the President:

"I do not really know whom to contact for this matter, but I have been asked to call your attention to the fact that Carlos Quirino, historian-writer, is 87 and deserves to get a National Artist Award before he dies.

"Nominated for the Award for Literature category, he was eliminated from 18 nominees when the nominees were short listed down to two writers, NVM Gonzalez and F. Sionel Jose, who are deserving but are much younger than Carlos Quirino. Carlos Quirino lost on a technicality, that there is no specific award for 'historical writing' or 'biography,' the field to which Carlos Quirino devoted an entire lifetime and which are creative nonetheless, and relevant too in this time of the Centennial of the 1898 Revolution.

"Quirino has written books on Philippine history, biographies of heroes and presidents and hundreds of published articles. One book made him the first and only Filipino to be invited as a Fellow of the Royal Geographic Society of Great Britain in the early 1970s Philippine Cartography, a reference book for old Philippine maps. See the enclosed compendium of his works.

"To avoid the lobbying that attends these Awards, perhaps you may submit to the National Commission on Culture and Arts and the Cultural Center of the Philippines a suggestion either to create a Special Category for Historical Writing or to create a Lifetime Achievement Award for Quirino's whole body of work. This will adequately reward a great historian who wrote so much about Aguinaldo, Rizal and the events that led to the 1898 revolution, the centennial of which we are now celebrating. Historian Carlos Quirino contributed much to the building of our nation, since he started to write in the days of Quezon up to today."

On October 12,1997, President Ramos responded by writing to the Quirino family, saying, "I also created a new category – the National Artist Award for Historical Literature and Mr. Carlos Quirino, Sr. has been chosen, for his outstanding contribution in this literary field, as the first recipient of this title and award." The bold face and underlining is the President's. And at the back, having been a neighbor of the Quirinos, hose only a block from his own, and added in his writing, "Mr. Charlie Quirino, Sr. and family – Congratulations."

I am proud to say Charlie is related to my late wife, and is the source of my articles on the skeletons in the closets of the Ayalas and the Cojuangcos. He really deserves the Award. I hate to have to write about assholes who don't deserve it.

Part 2. A naked encounter

Carlos Quirino is the favorite uncle of my late wife Cecilia Lichauco, who insists on my calling him "cousin" because he feels much younger than I do.

And he feels young because he has brought into his own life and into others, a dimension of immortality that comes with being a historian, one who writes about Filipinos past from the beginning of time, and whose writings will be read by Filipinos yet unborn to the end of time. A man who deals with immortality feels forever young.

Historian Carlos Quirino is probably the last of a generation. He is a Bataan veteran, dapper aide to President Elpidio Quirino, great lover thrice married, pursued by women so numerous they can only be counted by the Bureau of Census and Statistics. His third and last wife is Liesl Commans, authoress of "Why the Great Balls of fire if I am Going Pffft Anyway?", who we suspect fitted him with a chastity belt and forced him to concentrate on writing biographies and historical pieces. He is the author of 28 books, ranging from biographies of Young Aguinaldo and Amang Rodriguez, to sagas of the Cojuangco and the Ayala-Zobel families, which are unpublished perhaps because in his passionate search for truth, he unearthed too many family skeletons.

In 1940, young Carlos Quirino competed in a government contest for a biography of Dr. Jose Rizal, vying with such great authors as Camilo Osias and Rafael Palma. He lost, of course. Then he was called by the President Manuel L. Quezon to Malacañang and was ushered to the President's bedroom where the great Quezon stood completely naked, ready to put on his clothes. Quezon, in his birthday suit, faced him and said, "I read all the entries and I think yours is the best. Here's P3,000, the equivalent of First Prize. Keep it to your self. I don't want to embarrass the judges."

This is the book The Great Malayan cited by Quezon as the best biography of Rizal, first published in 1946 and re-published today 50 years later, to be launched October 28 in the former Nielson Tower, corner Ayala and Makati Avenue. Well, how did Carlos Quirino react when he first met Quezon? He was flattered and greatly honored of course but his greatest impressions came from the unforgettable sight of President Ouezon, completely naked, built like a horse and truly a national treasure for the women of his generation.

Last month on September 5, 1997, I wrote a memo to President Ramos suggesting a new category of Historical Writing be created for the National Artist Award, to honor Carlos Quirino and the many historians and biographers who gave us Filipinos a sense of national identity, especially in view of the coming Centennial Celebration of the 1898 Revolution. The President, God bless him, responded a month later on October 12 with an announcement that a new category of Historical Literature, no less important and no less creative than Fiction and Poetry, has been created and Carlos Quirino is indeed the first recipient of this title and award. Congratulations, Uncle Charlie.

On December 8 this year, at the Ceremonial Hall of Malacañang Palace, President Ramos will personally confer this honor on Carlos Quirino. As Presidential Consultant on National Affairs, I have been authorized to inform Mr. Quirino that unlike President Quezon, President Ramos will be fully clothed.

Part 3. Carlos Quirino, the man

National Artist Historian Carlos Quirino, 87, is probably the last of a generation.

He was born in Manila even before the First World War, on January 14, 1910, and fought in Second World War in Bataan, earning the Purple Heart after being shot in the ass while jumping into a ditch. He was in the Philippine Army (1941-46) under General Dug-out Doug MacArthur, and was incorporated into the 2nd Regular Division of USAFFE forces that surrendered in Bataan. He was forced to walk from Bataan to Capas in the infamous Death March. After his escape in a cane field and a bout with malaria, he joined the guerrilla band called President Quezon's Own Guerrillas (PQOG), all throughout the Japanese Occupation. He came out of the war as a colonel, and served as aide-de-camp to his cousin President Elpidio Quirino (1945-50). And in 1990 he was awarded the Philippine Legion of Honor (Degree of Officer) by President Corazon Aquino.

His father Dr. Jose F. Quirino, a Berlin-educated gynecologist, driving his new car on a picnic to Antipolo with his family, lost control of the car and drove it into a ravine. The wooden steering wheel broke and pierced his heart. The four year old Carlos was to remember years later the sudden death of his 33-year old father, and the sight of him lying deathly pale in the light of the full moon at the back of a carretela on its way to town.

His early death left a beautiful widow with two orphaned boys, Felix and the younger Carlos, only 4 years old. The mother Dolores (called Tia Lolita) lived in General Luna Street and had properties for rent, with enough income to send Carlos to La Salle (HS'27), abroad to University of Wisconsin (BA in journalism '31), Philippine Law School (LLB '41).

In 1940 he was National Rifle Champion, one of the best in Asia. In 1943, he passed the bar, and became a full-fledged lawyer. His schools acknowledged him proudly as their own. In 1960 he received the Distinguished Service Award from the University of Wisconsin, where he formed long and lasting friendships with TV anchormen Harry Reasoner, Walter Cronkite and Bob de Haven whose book "55 Years Behind the

Mike" became an American classic and set the standards for broadcasting. In 1977, as a Golden Jubilarian of De La Salle University, he received the Lifetime Achievement Award from the Alumni Association. In 1987, La Salle gave him the "Diamond Jubilarian Loyalty Tribute."

At the age of 22, he was a reporter of the Philippine Herald (1932-36) and at 24, he was the first Filipino foreign correspondent of the United Press International (UPI). He joined the Philippine Book Guild as its business manger (1937-41). Then he joined the government and became a public servant, as technical assistant in the Department of the Interior (1937-41), administrator of the Department of Commerce (1955-59) and director of the National Library (1961-65).

But Carlos Quirino's greatest fascination is for books as man's best teachers and most faithful friends. He became chairman of the Filipiniana Book Guild (1966-70, 1976-80), founding curator of the Ayala Museum and Library (1965-72), chairman of the International Association of Historians of Asia (1970-74) and senior associate editor of the 10-volume Filipino Heritage in 1978.

During the Rizal Centennial year 1961, Carlos Quirino was highly commended for his services as editor-in-chief of Rizal in Retrospect; for his meritorious Filipiniana Collection (maps in particular) by the Book Lovers Society and awarded the List Prize for his exhibition of rare books, also during the Rizal Centennial. Twice he received the highest commendation from the Philippine Historical Association, in 1973 and 1975. He was finalist of the 1987 Gintong Aklat Award of the Book Development Association and the Madrigal Memorial Foundation. In the same year he was made knight commander of the Distinguished Order of Quezon.

Carlos Lozada Quirino: soldier, shooter, lover, writer, National Artist.

Part 4. Is biography writing literature?

I don't intend to quarrel with misplaced accountants, ex-Central Bank governors and their hired hacks and paid pipers who decry lobbyists for the National Artists Awards and spread rumors that Senator Leticia Shahani will exert influence to have the Award for Historical Literature taken away from Carlos Quirino.

Fie on them. But I will take exception to views expressed by colleagues Adrian Cristobal Cruz of the Philippine Daily Inquirer, who are honest and without malice in their opinions that biography and historical writing is not part of literature.

Webster's Unabridged Dictionary, Third Edition, defines literature as "writings in prose or verse; especially writings having excellence of form or expression and expressing ideas of permanent or universal interest." And this is not limited, as Adrian Cristobal Cruz contends it is, to novel, essay, poetry and playwriting. It covers all kinds of writing, including historical writing and biographies.

For goodness sake, if people are uncomfortable with the term "Historical Literature," let's have it changed to what I suggested to President Ramos in the first place, "Historical Writing and Biography."

My source, Adrian and Neal, is the Encyclopedia Britannica, 1947 edition, which is the best of all editions, the later ones having mostly shortened articles of universal knowledge. How much more authoritative than that can we get?

"Literature, a general term which, in default of precise definition, may stand for the best expression of the best thought reduced to writing." Volume 14, Page 206C (lower right side), under Literature.

"Biography, that form of history which is applied, not to races or masses of men, but to an individual." Volume 3, Page 593D (lower right side), under Biography.

All written works are judged on style, substance, creative imagination and universal truth (even in fiction). Literature is usually divided into prose and poetry, fiction and non-fiction. Among the prose and non-fiction are categorized "best expression of the best thoughts reduced to writing" in the field of historical writing like Edward Gibbon's literary masterpiece The Decline and Fall of the Roman Empire, biographies like Boswell's Samuel Johnson and Plutarch's Lives which are considered great literature. I myself admire the excellence of style and substance of Leon Ma. Guerrero's biography of Rizal, The First Filipino, Horacio de la Costa's Light Cavalry and Claro M. Recto's and Teodoro Locsin Sr.'s many literary endeavors.

Carlos P. Romulo, who was neither a poet nor a fiction writer (whose two "novels" are relatively unknown), not even a historian or a biographer, but a journalist, was given the National Award for Literature. We can do no less for Carlos Lozada Quirino, our greatest living biographer and historian, who helped give the Filipino a sense of self-worth especially in today's national identity crisis, at the time when we are celebrating the Centennial of our Republic.

Many of the gripes we read about are from minor artists who think that the National Artist Awards are exclusively theirs to be distributed among themselves even without merit, as part of "the judgment of their peers." That is a lot of bull. There is more envy and jealousy, more back-biting and self-praise, more complaints, more lobbying for honors among artists than in any other group. It has been so before and even more so today, when many of them challenge the very rationale for these government awards.

Part 5. Quirino's works

He belonged to a remarkably handsome family. And he looked incredibly good looking in a white gold-braided army gala uniform, as an aide of his "cousin" President Elpidio Quirino, dancing with the First Lady, presidential daughter Vicky Quirino, in slinky silken sequined white gown, in many of those Malacañang balls.

My beautiful wife and his lovely niece Cecilia, part of his handsome family, would inevitably remark with a shake of her curly head, "Handsome sonamagun, isn't he? If my best friend Norma (elder sister of Vicky Quirino) were not killed during the war, she would be dancing there with him, glowing with a teenage crush."

Like the heroes he wrote about – Rizal, Aguinaldo, Quezon – National Artist Carlos Lozada Quirino was a great lover of women, suave, sophisticated, smooth, so much like Ateneans adept in writing poetic love letters in both English and Spanish and so unlike most of the La Salle *coño boys* of which he is one. When he became National Rifle Champion, women just swooned at the subconscious thought of his gunning for them with a weapon even more powerful and overwhelming.

In the course of time and circumstance, Uncle Charlie married three times, first to an American girl named Peggy Dawson; second to a stunningly beautiful girl Nena Bowen and last to a German Spanish mestiza Liesl Commans, and with them sired six children (Corny, Carlitos, Cecil, Denden, Caloy and Ritchie), 15 grandchildren and four great grandchildren. Liesl herself was an authoress of *Why the Great Balls of Fire* if I am *Going Phffft Anyway?*, a hilarious account of how she won the war over lthe Japanese occupation army, and *Like the Wind I Go*, an epic novel of three generations of Filipinos, about a Muslim who became the president of the Philippines, and about self redemption and self sacrifice in war-torn Vietnam, my *gulay*.

The historical writings of Carlos Lozada Quirino earned him the Cultural Heritage Award in 1961 and 1970, and the Father Horacio de la Costa Award for Historical Writing in 1978, and the Achievement Award of the National Research Council of the Philippines in 1987. One book made him the first and only Filipino to be invited as a Fellow of the Royal Geographic Society of Great Britain: *Philippine Cartography*, a reference book for old Philippine maps.

He wrote sagas of the Madrigal, Cojuangco and the Ayala-Zobel families, some of which are unpublished perhaps because in his passionate search for truth, he unearthed too many family skeletons. In his research, for instance, he discovered the origins of the fabulous wealth of the Cojuangco family.

One source was Melencio Cojuangco, grandfather of President Cory, business magnate Danding and PLDT's Ramon, who during the Philippine-American War, was forced to billet General Arthur MacArthur (father of Dug-out Doug) and his staff in his mansion in Paniqui, Tarlac. He offered his warehouses to store the American war material; and in return, Melencio was privileged to load his rice produce on the empty trains going back to Manila where the price was five times higher. He made a killing.

The other source was Melencio's sister, Ysidra, rumored to be the sweetheart of General |Antonio Luna, who was entrusted once by Luna with several carts of gold commandeered from the churches of Bulacan and Pampanga. These were to be temporarily stored in the Cojuangco warehouse while General

Luna left suddenly for Cabanatuan upon the telegraphed orders of President Aguinaldo and there he was cruelly assassinated. The Aguinaldo republic was defeated and the Americans inquired about the gold which they wanted to take over. Ysidra, according to Quirino's account, threw the gold into a we'll and recovered it later after the war ended.

Quirino also discovered the wonderful and fascinating story of why and how Doña Margarita Roxas de Ayala became the country's greatest benefactor and philanthropist of all time, and the real founding mother of the Zobel clan. It is a story just waiting to be told.

Critics who say that history is not literature are wrong. In 1953 Winston Churchill won the Nobel Prize for Literature for his four-volume *History of the English Speaking Peoples*. Also, his epic *History of the Second World War*. That's real history. That's great literature.

October 15 to 27, 1997, ISYU

Part 6. Eulogy for Carlos Quirino: soldier, shooter, lover, writer, National Artist

On May 20, 1999 Carlos Quirino died. On May 25 I delivered an eulogy in ceremonies held at the Cultural Center, starting with:

"National Artist Carlos Lozada Quirino is the favorite uncle of my late wife Cecilia Lichauco, who insisted on my calling him 'cousin' because he feels so much younger than I do. And he feels young because he has brought into his own life and into others, a dimension of immortality that comes with being a historian, one who writes about Filipinos past from the beginning of time, and whose writings will be read by Filipinos yet unborn to the end of time. A man who deals with immortality feels forever young."

And ending with:

"On December 8, 1997, another great President, Fidel V. Ramos, fully clothed and beaming with pride, personally conferred upon Carlos Quirino the honor of being the first National Artist Awardee in Historical Literature. Last May 20, 1999, as it comes to all men, Carlos Quirino passed away at the age of 89.

"Farewell, Uncle Charlie, we cannot hold you back any more than we can hold back the dawn, or youth, or love as it grows

and changes. For the best things in life are caught on the wing, and kept in some measure by letting them go.
"Farewell, Uncle Charlie, in our hearts you will never die."]
May 5, 1999 at the Cultural Center

ooooo

CHAPTER 3. Mayor, General, Presidential hopeful Alfredo Lim

Part 1. Lim achieved more than Ramos

Once my wife and I asked our compadre Eddie Ramos, then the chief of the Constabulary, to please get rid of a squatter who was subdividing and renting out our Parañaque property. Seven years passed and Eddie, despite the tremendous powers he had during the martial law era, could not dislodge the squatter in the light of what he called due process.

One day I saw General Alfredo Lim, National Bureau of Investigation (NBI) director during Cory's time, and asked him to please get rid of my pesky squatter. He simply said, "Tomorrow, he will be out." And Lord Almighty and his saints included, what Eddie Ramos could not do in seven years, Alfredo Lim did in single day. Since Eddie Ramos is my hero, it stands to reason that Alfredo Lim comes in a very close second.

Today we write a series of articles to take a measure of this remarkable man, whose moral courage and ability to get things done are worthy of the gods on Mount Olympus, and who now comes into the presidential fray as a man on horseback, like the cavalry to the rescue, man of the hour, man of the year, and it fortunes smiles upon him at this late stage, the man of the next six years and the next hundred years – the presidentiable Mayor of Manila, Alfredo Lim.

Last October, Metro Manila mayors were called to a whole day seminar on the government's anti-drug campaign. Alfredo Lim of Manila arrived half an hour before President Ramos was to open the seminar at four o'clock in the afternoon at Camp Ricardo Papa. He had not the slightest hunch that this attendance in that event would open the floodgate of media reports and commentaries about him as a presidential aspirant. The seminar participants were shooting a breeze while waiting for the arrival of the Chief Executive. The political babble suddenly bubbled when the legendary bulb flickered on Metro Manila Development Authority (MMDA) Chairman Prospero Oreta. On seeing Lim, Oreta blurted out a powerful suggestion that the mayor represent Metro Manila in the presidential contest. As if on cue, Secretary Dionisio Dela Serna seconded Oreta's motion. Taken aback by the strong persuasion, Lim could only insist that his only plan was to seek a third term at the city hall. Oreta then proposed a separate meeting to explore the possibility of a Lim presidency.

It came to pass that such a meeting was held, attended by 13 mayors, Oreta and dela Serna who started convincing Lim to join the LAKAS-NUCD. Lim refused to become a political butterfly, preferring to stick it out with People's Reform Party to which he has belonged since he entered politics and became Manila mayor. That meeting and of course, the agenda were on the front pages of the newspapers and in the headliners of broadcast news in no time at all.

Soon the persuasive show of support from friends and political acquaintances were snowballing. Lim began to seriously consider running for president. He denies having been given by Jaime Cardinal Sin a commitment of support. Lim visited the Manila archbishop and told him about the suggestions. Sin according to Lim, advised him to "carefully study the matter and I'll pray for you." And Lim, indeed, is an extremely cautious man. Military discipline had taught him to look before he leaps and he is not jumping into the presidential fray without first surveying the battlefield. Cautious of the fact that it is the highest national post he is being coaxed to aspire to, Lim still testing the waters. (More tomorrow)

Part 2. Fred Lim looking for a First Lady?

Presidential Mayor Fred Lim, a retired police general, a crack investigator, is verifying every single pledge of support he is receiving. He has also been going around the archipelago to find out for himself if his popularity is not limited to Metro Manila.

His fame did not go unnoticed by known political kingpins. Lim disclosed that Peping Cojuangko invited him to two meetings and, in both occasions, tried to convince him to join the presidential derby, promising him support. Cojuangko later announce in a press conference his all-out support for Gloria Macapagal's presidential bid and Lim has stayed away from the Cojuangko camp since then.

He says Gloria Macapagal Arroyo made a mistake accusing him of not declaring his San Francisco property in his statement of assets and liabilities, and saying that a house and lot were bought from Gloria's mother-in-law. Lim narrates that his family had rented the house, owned by a Taiwanese businessman for $800 a month since 1982 until the owner decided to sell the property in 1988. Because of the property's sentimental value to the Lim family, the owner agreed to sell it to them on an installment plan. His six children gainfully employed in the U.S. then, were paying the property. When Lim won P5,612,000 in a sweepstakes draw, the family paid the balance in full. Lim said the property declared in his statement of assets and liabilities.

Lim is presently determined not to turn his back on the People's Reform Party which, in 1992, tried but failed to talk him into becoming Miriam Santiago's running mate. He says his taking a shot at the presidential derby would depend on Miriam's plans. Last Monday, December 1, Miriam issued to Senate reports announcing her plan to invite Lim to be the PRP'S vice presidential candidate. Lim has earlier been quoted as saying that he would rather seek a third term as mayor if he decided not to join the presidential race.

If he becomes president, Lim's top priority would to give the citizens peace of mind through the restoration of peace and order in the land. He would see to it that laws are strictly enforced, that the citizens are equally protected and that there would no sacred cows to stand in the way of the fight against criminal elements.

As NBI director, Lim solved the murder of Maureen Haltman and sent to jail Claudio Teehankee, Jr. whose father, the late Supreme Court Justice Teehankee, Sr. was his compadre. Lim believes that where peace and order reign, there is political stability and that this brings economic prosperity. He is batting for the return to the old setup where the police force was under the direct control and supervision of local executives for a more effective drive against criminality.

He denies stories that he is in search of a wife so that the nation may have a First Lady if he is able to capture Malacañang. The widower says that the lady journalist teased him about having a first lady and he jokingly retorted that he wants someone who likes him because he would just be wasting time if he courts one and is rejected. He quips, "Baka naman sabihin sa akin, 'Ikaw naman, mayor, liligaw-ligaw ka pa, eh, ang tanda-tanda mo na.'" (More tomorrow)

Part 3. Lim's first experience with rights violation

Alfredo Siojo Lim grew up with his maternal grandparents in the Dapitan area, on Calle Alfredo. An only child, he was still in his mother's womb when his father died. His mother remarried and entrusted him to her parents. Lim has fond memories of his childhood. He was happy being the favorite grandchild.

The financial support his grandparents were receiving from their children provided ample means to satisfy his material demands, luxury items included. They had a maid who would take him to P. Gomez Elementary School and, at recess time, would buy him a bottle of Magnolia Chocolait, a status symbol in the pre-war era.

He vividly remembers an episode in his fourth grade, recollection of which makes him beam impishly. It was his turn to clean the classroom, an assignment given to public school pupil to this day. He asked his teacher that he be excused that day because he had a painful boil ripe for a Mount Pinatubo-like eruption. The teacher wouldn't budge, thinking he was just making an alibi. As he was husking the floor, the boil was punctured. Poor 10-year-old Alfredo went home crying. Angered by her pet grandchild's experience, his grandmother rushed to the school and berated the teacher, hurling invectives at her. The school principal tried to mediate but she, too, had to bear his grandmother's ire. Lim watched with a natural high over his first-ever victory against what present-day advocates brand as a form of a child abuse and human rights violation.

The comfortable life he was enjoying with his grandparents was disrupted by the war. Fierce fighting cut off the monetary support from his uncles and aunts. At 12, Lim had to sell rice cakes his grandmother baked to sustain them. Neighbors, attracted by a well-groomed boy peddling, would buy more than they could consume, and other ambulant vendors would eat their hearts out seeing the young Lim having disposed of his merchandise even before they could find their first customer. His grandmother died on April 10, 1943, a date Lim remembers every day of his life.

He was left to the care of his godmother, Dr. Dolores Lao Conde who, after the war, encouraged him to learn how to make a living. Lim got himself employed as a bus conductor. Those buses were ambulances converted into public utility vehicles plying the Blumentritt-Sta. Cruz and Quiapo-Divisoria routes. He later worked as a security guard and as a salesman, supporting himself through high school at the Far Eastern University and college at the University of the East where he finished Business Administration in 1951 and Law in 1963. He was already in the police force when he took up Law. He earned a master's degree in national security administration from the National Defense College of the Philippines where he graduated with honors in 1981.

He described himself as a "straight" boy, having been strictly disciplined even while being pampered by his grandparents from whom he learned the fundamentals of what is right and wrong. He was taught to honor God, help and respect others, obey the elders and be honest – the same kind of discipline he instilled in his own children. He says that he did not figure in school brawls and never was a campus bully.

Part 4. Proudly Dirty Harry

While in high school, Mayor Alfredo Lim read a lot of detective stories and became fascinated by the way policeman solved crimes and were hailed as a heroes. These inspired him to enter the police organization. He did in 1951 at the age of 22.

In the service, fellow cops taunted him for refusing to join them in nights out at girls bar but he insisted on clean living – no vices, not even smoking or drinking.

Lim has eight children, all living in the U.S. He first sent two of them and his wife there in 1980 due to death threats he started receiving then. His family would get a phone calls telling them to order a coffin for Lim. He suspects that the threats were the works of people he had to sent to jail. The rest of his children moved to the U.S. after finishing their studies. Lim is grandfather of 16 children.

Lim had a taste of bitter politics while in the police service. For 11 years, during the Marcos regime, he had to be content with being a lieutenant colonel. He was "kept in the freezer" by a political foes (then Mayor Ramon Bagatsing) of the late Mayor Antonio Villegas with whom he was said to be closely identified. He retired as a major General on December 21, 1989 and was appointed the following day by then President Cory Aquino as director of the NBI. He resigned from the post on March 23,1992 and was elected as mayor of Manila in May of the same year, enjoying the highest majority in the city's political history.

The policeman-turned-politician does not mind being dubbed as a Dirty Harry of the Philippines. To him, Dirty Harry, a movie based on the true story of a San Francisco detective-inspector, symbolizes a strong stand against all forms of criminality which, he said, should the attitude that lawmen must adopt if they are determined to assume the role of protectors of law-abiding citizens. He laughs at those who interpret the Dirty Harry label as a nickname for a "salvager." He dismisses insinuation that he resorts to "shortcuts" in running after criminal elements, stressing that he operates within the parameters of the law.

It was during stint at the NBI that he was persuaded to enter politics. He was a reluctant candidate in 1992, succumbing only a public clamor. He prefers to be a cop than a politician, saying that it is more self-fulfilling to solve a crime for that quenches the victims' thirst for justice. He had intended to bow out of public service as soon as he reached the mandatory retirement age in the police force, so he could be reunited with his family in the U.S. With his wife gone, he is married to his constituents, working at the city hall even on Saturdays and Sundays.

He is praised and criticized for his ability to get things

done fast. To his detractors, he explains that law enforces and government officials must be decisive and should not put off for tomorrow what can be done today because the people want immediate action on problems brought to their leaders' attention. He says it is better to act on a problem right away and rectify the errors that may be committed than to delay action or not do anything at all which are both tantamount to neglect of responsibility.

Part 5. Movie on President Lim starring Erap?

As NBI director, Fred Lim was responsible for the solution of the murder of Maureen Hultmann and the arrest of Claudio Teehankee, Jr. as the murderer. He was also responsible for the controversial 1990 drug operation against a group of military men which led to the resignation of Captain Jaylo from the force.

But the most heart-warming stories about Mayor Fred Lim are those of the people he helped without fanfare, without ever talking credit for it. I know of two cases that involve people I know. One of them is Luzviminda Sorilla, a beautician of my late wife, who was stricken with cancer of the breast which doctors said would have only three months to live. She lived three years instead undergoing chemical therapy and an experimental drug program under Dr. Emilio Abello, with financial support from Mayor Lim and friends. When her father had a heart attack and was confined in ICU for weeks, Mayor Lim was on hand to help.

Then there is the case of Josefina del Rosario, mother of a staff member, who went into a coma. Mayor Lim arranged to have her confined in the Ospital ng Maynila, free of charge. And when she finally died, Mayor Lim also subsidized her cremation and burial. These are but two of the many charities that Mayor Lim extends to hundreds of people who seek his help and financial support.

But perhaps the people would be more familiar with the story of Rona Mahilum, a young girl hailed as a heroine for having saved all the members of her family from a fire that gobbled up their house somewhere in Negros a year or two ago. She suffered severe burns during the heroic episode. Mayor Lim upon hearing the story, particularly that which said that she was not receiving ample medical treatment in the hospital in her province, personally fetched the girl and brought her to Manila for treatment of her burns. Mayor Lim also set up trust funds for Rona's education and other needs.

Except for Ramon Magsaysay, seldom in our political history do we encounter a man like Alfredo Lim – of humble and obscure beginnings who rose from the ranks by his own bootstraps without the faintest shadow or suspicion of anything remotely approaching a scandal impugning his integrity and honesty as a man and a public official, or his moral and physical courage in defense of what is right.

So colorful is his life that three movies were made of it – one starring Rudy Fernandez on his experiences as a cop (he met his wife when he frustrated a bag snatcher from victimizing her), another starring Ramon Revilla on his experiences as Manila's Chief of Police (wiping out scads of malefactors and criminals), and a third starring Eddie Garcia on his experiences as NBI Chief (most against drug lords, subversives and murderers for hire).

And soon we hope to see his fourth movie about Fred Lim starring the King of Movies himself Fernando Poe Jr. probably on his experiences as Mayor of Manila. Perhaps in the future we will also see a fifth movie based on his life as president of the Philippines, starring Erap Estrada himself, hahaha.

Go ahead, Mayor Lim, make my day.
December 11 to 17, 1997, ISYU

ooooo

CHAPTER 4. Padilla-Rufino

Part 1. For God's sake, pay up, Ernest Rufino!

RUTH Gallemit is one talented individual destined for success. Born to a humble family in a remote part of Zamboanga, the only girl among eight children, she dared to invade Manila all alone by herself.

She overcame the barriers of sex, of social position, of distance, to become a nurse, an employee of Carnation Philippines, of Mondragon where she was a cosmetologist promoted to Supervisor of the La Prairie division.

She counted as her clients such well-known personalities as Tina Monson Palma, Julie Daza, Patsy Gonzalez, Charo Yujuico, Dulce Saguisag, Tina Bernardo.

Ruth worked from 7 am to 7 pm daily, even on Sundays, and went nursing in the St. Claire Hospital on days off just to keep in practice. A petite, well-proportioned and pretty woman at the age of 30, still unmarried, Ruth Gallemit was the main support of her family in Zamboanga.

In January she became the nurse and secretary of my daughter-in-law dermatologist Dr. Vicki Belo-Henares who opened up a clinic for skin care, earning P7,000 a month plus commission that netted her P15,000 on her first month of employment. She was on the rise in the world of rich and beautiful people, with shining hopes, a bright future, and love's promise in the eyes of many suitors.

On February 24, she celebrated her 30th birthday in her apartment where she cooked a delicious meal for 80 of her friends, singing and dancing the night away.

The next night Vicki was called to the emergency room of the Makati Med, and there on the stretcher lay Ruth, her scalp torn off her skull and kept in place by an improvised hair net, air tubes sticking out of her mouth, intravenous lines carrying vital fluids into her bloodstream. A CT scan showed her brain like mashed potatoes.

At 5:30 am, Ruth Gallemit was dead, and with her died all the hopes of youth, great expectations of her parents, and love's promise.

Ruth and her friends celebrated February Revolution on the EDSA Disco ng Kalye. About midnight, the group walked along the Edsa towards her Bliss Apartment in Guadalupe. Afraid of being accosted by hoodlums on the unlit overpass, they decided to cross Edsa near Boni Avenue.

Suddenly a Nissan car speeding southward hit Ruth on the pelvis, making her spin over in midair and land on her skull ten meters away from the point of impact.

The driver, Ernest Rufino III, 23 year old son of Ernest Jr. did not even bother to stop to pick up the accident victim, a clear case of hit-and-run.

Both father and son, Junior and Ernest III, showed up later at the hospital to admit that the boy hit Ruth, with security guards armed with armalites, and *kunyari* taking charge of getting the best doctors to care for the victim -- only when all is said and done, they were not around to pay the bills.

The parents of the driver Ernest III are multi-billionaires -- his grandfather Ernie Rufino Sr. was the pioneer in movie theaters, and at one time had a stranglehold on all first-run Hollywood movies except MGM -- and his other grandfather, Senator Ambrosio Padilla, is of a family from Pangasinan known for great wealth and an even greater reluctance to part with a single centavo of it.

So the Rufinos disappeared and in their stead came a supercilious lawyer named Atty. Alejandro de la Rosa. He won't entertain representations from Vicki or any of Ruth's friends who were stuck with the settling of bills for doctors and funeral.

This lawyer kept repeating that Senator Padilla has taken interest in the case (to impress, no doubt). He also insisted that the poor parents of Ruth come to Manila from far Zamboanga for a talk. They came without money, and this multi-billionaire Rufino kept them waiting for two weeks without even offering to pay for their room and board, and had the temerity to inform them that all he is prepared to do is to help them collect the insurance money!

Phoenix Insurance (the insurer) is run by Norma Alvendia, best friend of Ruth, so no help is needed on that score. Clients like Patty Claparols, Fe Chua, and others gave P30,000. Another P30,000 came from by Vicki and Atom Henares. No Rufino came to the wake or offered condolences.

But Ernest Rufino Jr. cannot be disturbed because he flew to the USA "for a medical check-up."

The parents of Ruth said from the beginning that they are not interested in suing the young boy who killed their daughter, and would have been content to receive any little help given. All they got is uncaring arrogance.

My advice to them is to get a big-shot lawyer on a contingency fee basis, and sue the hell out of Ernest III, to show what justice has in store for the hit-and-run driver who has all the wealth in the world but no heart for his fellow man.
April 14, 1989, Philippine Daily Inquirer

Part 2. Josie Padilla Rufino to Oscar Eguia

DEAR Mr. Eguia, your open letter answering my response to Larry Henares' column, is a masterful tapestry of lies, contradictions, and allegations on matters you know nothing about and/or have deliberately misread.

Your clincher is most effective, "I was there. You were not." This is exactly the point. You were not at the place you claim to be. You claim now that the accident happened in front of Citytrust. In fact, the accident happened in front of Gascor immediately after the corner of Boni Avenue at EDSA. This is very clear from the official investigation report, conducted and prepared that very night by Cpl. Agripino Lloret, based on witnesses' accounts which included your own companions.

How can you lie so blatantly about something so evident! Are you now also calling your own companions liars?

Nevertheless, I note that you realize the gravity of crossing a national highway where railings are put up precisely to stop people from doing so. I also note that you do not deny the existence of an overpass and that you also were crossing where it was obviously prohibited.

Your letter is full of contradictions. You write, "As we started to cross, there was no car close enough to hit us. But this car was running so fast that before we realized it, it was already upon us." If this were true, then all of you would have been hit!

While you claim that the car was running so fast, you also claim that one of you noted the license plate. It is unbelievable that someone could note the license plate of a car you claim you did not even see coming, and at 1:20 AM! The truth, as you very well know, Mr. Eguia, is that Ernie stopped his car immediately after the incident.

You claim that the first time you saw Ernie was at the hospital one hour later, implying that he only arrived at that time, further implying that it was "hit and run." Again let me refute you based on the hospital guard's official report which stated that the accident happened at approximately 1:20 AM. By 1:50 AM, the guard had reported the accident to the Mandaluyong police, already complete with Ernie's name, address, license plate and plate number.

Obviously, Ernie was present to supply all these information; even you can only claim to the license number being noted. How could Ernie have given this information to the guard within the half hour if you claim he was there one hour later?

You also claim that it was Atom and Vicki Henares who helped raise money for all the expenses. At the same time, you say the hospital bill remains unpaid. Which is it?

The fact is that the next day after the accident, we had written the insurance company "to settle with the family of the deceased." We were confident that an early payment could be released to the Gallemits, considering our express consent, the professional integrity of Phoenix Insurance, and the fact that its President's wife was the best friend of the deceased.

Unfortunately, Mr. Atom Henares blocked this early payment of P70,000 to the Gallemits. I quote from the insurance company's status report to us, "Mr. Henares inquired about the limits of liability under the policy. When we informed him, he insinuated that the maximum coverage will not be enough to settle the claim considering that the deceased was earning no less than P20,000 a month." In said letter, the insurance company has stated that "we are ready, willing and able to meet our liability under our policy as soon as an agreed settlement is reached."

Mr. Atom Henares blocked this settlement, and then he and his wife Vicki went on to play hero about trying to raise money for the expenses.

Aside from your contradictions, you misread (deliberately) what I have written and then attack me for it. For example, you say, "It is an absolutely lie... that your son helped load Ruth's body into the army jeep..." In fact I made no such statement; this exists only in your fertile imagination. What I wrote was, "A military jeep had also stopped. They loaded her in the jeep, and Ernie followed them to the hospital." Obviously, "they" and "them" refer to people other than Ernie.

I also note that you sound off on things you do not know anything about. You say "It is a lie that Dra. Vicki Belo Henares was demanding and threatening." Why, Mr. Eguia, were you ever present in a meeting between Vicki and our representatives? You say our lawyer was "arrogant and name dropping." You have never even met, much less talked to our lawyer, Atty. Alex de la Rosa.

`We note a deliberate attempt on your part to portray a dear family friend, Atty. Alex de la Rosa, as a heavy in this drama. The plain fact is this: Alex could not have made up the threats of Vicki, for they were in fact realized in Larry Henares' column. "Pay P350,000 or we'll put you all over the papers," she demanded and threatened. We didn't pay. Her father-in-law put us all over his column.

Even the computation is hers. She said nurse Ruth received P15,000 a month from her, so we must pay P350,000 to approximate her 2-year compensation (her original demand was P540,000 for a 3-year compensation. Note the discrepancies in their claims with Vicki claiming P15,000 and her husband Atom claiming she earned P20,000 a month). No, Mr. Eguia, Atty. Alex de la Rosa wasn't arrogant, he was indignant.

The irony here is that if Ernie were in any way at fault, paying off would have been the easy way out! But precisely because Ernie was innocent, and acted responsibly both before and after the accident, we are repelled by the lies, threats and demands made by Vicki Henares.

The only positive thing about your letter is it has finally revealed to us where we can get in touch with the Gallemits directly, and this contact has been made. Before this, the only response we could get for our efforts was Vicki's "We are the official spokesmen. We are the ones to be spoken to." We were given the impression that Ruth's parents had gone home.

This has been a most difficult letter to write. Your letter was so diabolical in its lies. It evoked much anger and caused much suffering.   I am trying hard to understand and sympathize with your sorrow, your regret, even your guilt which makes it so much easier to heap the blame on a stranger.

But this incident was an accident. Even in your cruelty you cannot deny this. But what you are doing and saying to destroy lives and reputations is most coldly deliberate and calculating. To what end, Oscar Eguia?

P.S. As soon as Mr. Eguia published an address where

the Gallemits could be reached, the Rufinos sent a representative to them. This representative was told they were not staying in the address Mr. Eguia claimed them to be, but in Marikina. They were reached in Marikina and a meeting was set for the Rufinos and the Gallemits for April 30. On the night of April 29th, the Gallemit lawyers canceled the meeting.

(Signed) JOSIE PADILLA RUFINO

May 20, 1989, Philippine Daily Inquirer

Part 3. From Atom Henares to Josie Padilla Rufino

DEAR Ms. Padilla Rufino, I refrained from answering your libelous accusations in two letters to the Inquirer because you are not in full possession of the facts, since you were neither there when your son caused the death of Ruth Gallemit, nor have you directly participated in subsequent discussions. I doubt if your statements can even be admitted in court, or survive cross examination.

I also refrained because of my high regard and respect for the Rufino family, many of whom are my good friends and whom I have always known to be generous and caring.

I also felt that you were too emotionally concerned about the reputation of your son, who appears to be incapable of speaking for himself.

Your repeated reference to the role Vicki and I played in this incident now forces me to respond.

My wife and I have never been authorized to negotiate for the Gallemits. We had only been asked to assist in the discussions. I made that clear to Atty. de la Rosa and Phoenix Insurance the first time I met with them. The insurance report you mischievously quoted in part indicates that.

Said the report: ``In accordance with the heirs' instruction, we contacted Mr. Atong (sic) Henares at his office to pursue our negotiation to settle the claim. He advised he still has to confer with the elders of the deceased when they come back from Zamboanga after the burial.''

Does that in any way imply I have taken charge of the case? The fact is that at that point, I had not even met the Gallemits.

I note that you used the same technique of truncating

quotations to fit your purposes in answering Mr. Eguia's letter. You denied that you said your son helped load Ruth's body into the army jeep, saying that "they" referred to other people.

While it is too true that Ernie did not help load Ruth's body into the jeep, it is also true that your account strongly implied he did. Let the reader decide for himself:

"Immediately after she was hit, Ernie stopped and got out of his car. A military jeep had also stopped. They loaded her in the jeep, and Ernie followed them to the hospital." Does not that suggest that Ernie stopped and got out, just as the people in the military jeep did -- and that THEY (both Ernie and the others) loaded the body into the jeep?

The second time I met Atty. de la Rosa, I was with the Gallemits who were there to negotiate for themselves. The third time, the Gallemits refused to come and sent Vicki to receive your token offer.

In any case, let me point out that:

The issue is not who caused the death of Ruth Gallemit -- because even your son admits to that.

The issue is not the details of the accident -- for that is for the courts to decide.

The issue is not about who paid for Ruth's hospital and funeral expenses -- because even you admit that you have not.

The issue is not the arrogance of Alex de la Rosa -- because the Gallemits themselves were so offended by his attitude that they immediately sought the legal advice of their nephew after their first and only meeting with your lawyer.

The issue is not Ruth's salary -- because she has signed a contract of employment for P7,000 a month plus 30 percent of net profits of the clinic. Ruth was more than Vicki's nurse, she was a partner.

The issue is not your inability to contact the Gallemits -- as the Gallemit's lawyer/nephew had contacted your husband directly on April 6 and was responded to by the Padilla law office in writing on April 11, three days before my father's article first appeared.

The issue is not whether the insurance company will pay -- because your consent is needed for the release of any insurance benefits, and you have been using this as a bargaining lever.

What the issue is, Ms. Padilla Rufino, is your reluctance to pay anything out of your own pocket to compensate the Gallemits for the loss of Ruth's life.

Your brother Alex has since reiterated your initial offer to merely "assist in the collection of the insurance" and add only an additional P30,000. This offer was however contingent on a recantation of all Mr. Eguia's and Mr. Henares' statements. Both Mr. Gallemit and his lawyer told Alex that these conditions are improper and unacceptable.

Ms. Padilla Rufino, it took only two days for you to respond to my father's article from Belmont, California. It has been close to three months since your son caused the death of Mr. Gallemit's daughter, and still you have not settled with the Gallemits, much less personally condoled with them.

They are still awaiting word from you. Will you now meet with the Gallemits and fairly compensate them for the loss of Ruth?

Or are you going to write another letter to the newspapers?

May 22, 1989, Philippine Daily Inquirer

Part 4. The Equalizer: a bit of human compassion

THE TV series, "The Equalizer," is about a retired intelligence officer who advertises in the newspaper, "If you are poor, helpless and hopeless, unable to cope with forces more powerful than you, I might be able to help you. Signed: The Equalizer."

That is what I try to be, an Equalizer. I do not pretend to be fair to the Americans, goodness knows they have their fine points. But there are hundreds of hired hacks, paid pipers and slime-balls like the Neuter from Nowhere who promote their LIC bloodbath doctrine, anti-industrialization IMF policy, and anti-nationalist posture -- so I try to equalize the struggle by speaking in behalf of Filipino nationalists, students, peasants, priests and nuns who are being killed for loving their country more than Mommie Dearest America.

I have championed the causes of the little people against penny-pinching miserly oligarchs with not an ounce of human compassion, who directly or indirectly abuse them, and take refuge in legal maneuvers and righteous hysterics to avoid their moral obligations. Remember Mrs. Chita Bito who was burned by a leaking Meralco transformer? And Mrs. Anicia Mejia whose daughter was killed by a PASVIL bus? And Rosario Baluyot?

I figure that between the very rich and the very poor there is no equality in life and before the law.

The rich are billionaires, with more than enough wealth to last them through twenty lifetimes. The poor live from hand to mouth, never knowing where the next meal is coming from.

The rich have all the connections with the police, the best lawyers, judges and powers-that-be, and the resources to keep a law case going for years on end. The poor are all alone in this city and in the hostile world, with no resources to protect their rights in the courts.

The rich can travel abroad, spending P500,000 a month for months on end if need be, but they refuse to part with a single centavo as a gesture of human compassion to the poor. The poor can pursue their case in Manila only through the charity of others.

When will the balance sheet be balanced? by whom? how?

Thus I feel impelled to take up their case, because there are very few they can turn to for help. I never needed any prodding from anyone, not even my family. Don't ever impute ulterior motives to me.

I am the Equalizer.

Years ago, a young man was driving northward along Edsa just beyond the Guadalupe bridge, when this child (who just came from a carnival fair at Shaw) darted across his path and got hit. He stopped his car, picked up the victim, and brought him to the Polymedic Hospital.

The young man assured the hospital authorities that he will pay for all expenses and insisted that the child be given immediate attention by the best available doctors.

An hour later, the parents of the child, who were very poor, came, and with them he drove to the Mandaluyong police station to report the accident.

At this point the young man called his parents to say he was involved in a serious accident, but that they should not get involved because he himself will take full responsibility.

The next day he went to Rico Insurance, coincidentally owned by the Alvendias who also own the Phoenix Insurance.

There he reported the accident to his Uncle Felicing Alvendia, and brought the insurance representative to the hospital and police station.

He got the insurance company to settle right away, but not satisfied with the amount, he paid much more out of his own pocket in addition to the insurance proceeds. When his father remonstrated with him, he said, "It is not a matter of rights or obligations. Just a bit of human compassion, Papa. These people are really poor."

Not only that, he visited the child every day for two weeks, paid all the bills, and personally drove him home. The parents were thankful and they never had any reason to sue in spite of ambulance chasers disguised as lawyers.

At that time he was only twenty years of age. And he never involved his parents or grandparents in his problem. He resolved it himself.

"Whether it was my fault or not, I caused injury to a poor child of indigent parents, with no resources to secure medical help or to seek legal recourse. The presumption is that I had full control of the car, and that I could see ahead far enough to avoid hitting that child.

"I am not criminally liable. But I believe I have a moral obligation, given the fact that I have more than enough resources and the victim's family has none, to help in the medical expenses of the child I ran over, and to commiserate with them in their hour of distress."

This young man went on to Harvard, to be an executive of a Multinational and a businessman in his own right.

He is my son Atom Henares, and I am proud to be his father.

May 29, 1989, Philippine Daily Inquirer

Part 5. Scrooge's wallet creaks with cobwebs (a reprise)

MY grandfather, the Grand Old Man of Pangasinan, once brought me to the house of a family friend. He warned me to empty my bladder before I entered the house -- but I just did not feel like.

Much later I asked the owner of the house, a legal luminary destined for the Supreme Court, for permission to use the bathroom. He brought me there and pointed to a cardboard pinned to the wall, "You know what this is? It is a scoreboard. You make four vertical lines and a diagonal to complete the set of five, you know, like they do in election contests."

"Yes," I answered, "but what does that got to do with what I have to do in the bathroom?"

"Well, in this house, when you make pee-pee, you make a mark -- but you do not flush the toilet until you make the diagonal!"

In other words, the pee-pee is done five times before the water is flushed down the toilet. "What for?" I asked.

"To save on water, of course," he answered. Well, he also saved on air, because I had to hold my breath in that bathroom.

My grandfather said this particular family from my province of Pangasinan has the reputation of being extremely *kuripot* -- a reputation that persists even to this day.

Charles Dickens described them perfectly as Ebenezer Scrooge in "A Christmas Carol," and Fagin in "Oliver Twist." Shakespeare wrote of them as Shylock who insists on his pound of flesh.

Ebenezer Scrooge come in family sizes you know -- the skin-flints, the tightwads, the penny-pinchers -- the miserly, stingy, niggardly, ungenerous, ungiving.

You go out with them on a double-date, and they go to the toilet when the bill is presented for payment. They rarely open their wallets, and when they do, you could hear the creaking of Dracula's door amidst a cloud of dust and cobwebs.

They rarely give Christmas gifts, even among their family -- and when they do, it is some unused item they received on their wedding day twenty years ago. And they rarely if ever contribute to charity or to the church, closing their eyes in fervent prayer whenever the collection plate is passed in front of them.

They scrimp and save, buy second-hand cars, eat the cheaper cuts of meat, live in modest homes and avoid going to concerts and stage plays just to preserve the family fortune they inherited and could never earn by their own ability -- which is admirable in some ways.

But when it comes to settling their obligations, they do so only when bananas start to grow in the North Pole and hell freezes over.

To Scrooge it is an eternal game of hide-and-seek, sneaking out the back door when the creditor comes to call; disguising his voice over the phone to say he is not home; leaving word that he is in a hospital or abroad for a medical check-up; pleading for time till the next payday.

And thousands of other alibis honed to perfection through generations for the purpose of welching on obligations.

In the final confrontation, they take refuge in every device to avoid paying. They pretend to be insulted, wax indignant over some imagined offense, screaming to all and sundry that they are being cheated, blackmailed, intimidated, and that they refuse to pay under threats. They will dare you to sue them, especially if there are lawyers in their family or among friends willing to work for free.

All of that of course is sham, because they never intend to pay in any case under any circumstances. They accuse people of trying to squeeze them out of their money, but it is evident to all that it is far easier to get $10 billion from Imelda than to pry one single centavo from their tightly closed fists.

Ah but the righteous indignation, the screaming hysterics, the howling histrionics, the Greek chorus of tearful recriminations that they are being robbed, cheated and blackmailed -- enough to make anyone who knows their stingy parsimonious nature throw up or head for the hills and join the communists.

Another Scrooge I know comes from the South, from my own province of Negros Occidental. He never pays his debts, and is so greedy that when his tenants make money, he throws them out of his building and gets into the same business in the same location himself.

Once he contracted to buy a Montalban property from a friend of mine, neglected to pay the required deposit, and sued my friend for not honoring the sale. He bribed the lower courts to "let him win the first and second rounds, as a sporting gesture because he will lose in the Supreme Court anyway." He boasted that while the case is in court, my friend could not sell the property -- and after years of litigation, my friend settled.

Friends, light candles to the Lord and pray that if

anyone owes you money, or rents your house, or treats you to dinner, or runs over your kid -- it won't ever be Ebenezer Scrooge!
June 1, 1989, Philippine Daily Inquirer

Part 6. Yellow, let mellow; brown, let it drown!

WELL, today we are supposed to continue our series on Danding Cojuangco, but we decided to do it later after the coup d'etat attempt is finally resolved. So if he is available, give us a call. Our series goes on with or without the interview.

"If it's yellow, let it mellow. If it's brown, let it drown." It sounds like the campaign slogan for the Cory Crusaders, most of whom were mestizas, insulares and peninsulares looking with some disdain at dark brown Filipinos. But in fairness to them, it is not.

It is the slogan of a prominent family in Pangasinan, of legal luminaries, of tremendous inherited wealth, and an enduring reputation for being stingy and miserly. They are big family so you must have met some of them. Many of them studied in Ateneo and stories by their classmates abound.

They are the ones who are reluctant to reach for the check when they join you for dinner. If you happen to pick up a 50-centavo coin near where they are standing, they will claim it as their own and will go after you with hammer and tongs for its possession.

If you dun them for a legitimate obligation, they will hem and haw and scream to high heavens that they are being subjected to highway robbery. If they happen to run over your child, do not even bother to sue; they are a family of lawyers and hell will freeze over before they will part with a single centavo aside from the insurance money. You know the type.

Appropriately displayed over their toilet seats, their slogan in another version easier to understand, reads: "If it's yellow, let it smell-o. If it's brown, flush it down." That's how they save on their water bill.

You should be curious what happens when you flush it down. The water closet spills out its contents into the toilet bowl, creating a whirlpool that swirls counter-clockwise here above the equator in the northern hemisphere; in Australia below the equator, it moves clockwise. It is called Corialis

Effect.

Then it is flushed down through a U-tube which serves as a water lock to keep bad odors from coming up from the sewers. Down the drain it goes till it falls into a septic tank called *poso negro*.

The poso negro is made up of two chambers: the Digesting chamber and the Leaching chamber. The solid brown waste settles to the bottom of the Digestive chamber, while the water is drained from the top to the Leaching Chamber. From there it leaves the septic tank to go the sewer drains. a *siñgao* air pipe relieves the air pressure like the holes in a can of milk, so the liquid can flow freely.

The sewers may lead to a waste treatment plant where the water may be chemically treated to remove bacteria and pollutants, and then poured into the sea.

Back to the septic tank, pretty soon it is full of dung and has to be emptied. Chances are, for this service, we will call one of the Malabanan family, who for three generations, made their fortunes excavating septic sludge from septic tanks.

This family business was started by Melencio Malabanan in 1970, with his children: Leopoldo, Priscilla, Rodolfo, Carmelita, and Angela. They sold the sludge to Laguna farmers as fertilizer for P25 per truckload.

Today, there are at least 15 separate Malabanan firms manned by children and grandchildren, listed on page 527 of the latest PLDT white page directory.

Well, what the heck, we ain't beaten yet. We'll flush out those rebels out Makati for sure, because when all is said and done, we have a secret and ultimate weapon, devised exclusively by Filipinos.

It consists of following the advice of the little woman who called up on DZRH to give our Armed Forces a few pointers way back in January 1987 during the siege of Channel Seven. In her high pitched voice this master strategist and tactician exclaimed:

"Primero, putulin ninyo ang tubig. Pag hindi pa sumuko, putulin ninyo and ilaw. Pag hindi pa mag surrender, pasabogan ninyo ng Malabanan!"

Just imagine some 150 pump trucks of the Malabon Family aiming a barrage at Hotel Nikko Manila Gardens on Pasay Road, and also at the American Embassy on Roxas

Boulevard, drowning them in brown matter, until at last Gringo Honasan and his mutineers, as well as Ambassador Kulas Platypus, Ken Quinn, CIA spooks Billygoat Lofgren and Stevedore Perry emerge, marching out to surrender under a white flag of toilet tissue paper!

Ah, 'tis a consummation devoutly to be wished!

With such weaponry, we Filipinos can liberate the Philippines from our colonial masters and their pro-consuls in the military and the Council of Trent.

Then tomorrow, by golly, we shall conquer the world!

December 7, 1989, Philippine Daily Inquirer

[Nota Bena, 2002: The Padillas sued Larry Henares for damages in the Pasig Regional Trail Court. He was acquitted.]

ooooo

CHAPTER 5. Jaime Zobel de Ayala

Part 1. Full are the heavens and the earth!

STANLEY SCHRAGER of the US Embassy who would look like Robert Redford if he was not shoved into a meat grinder, remarked at the Cultural Center the other night, "Larry, you are getting soft," referring of course to the temporary lull on browbeating the Americans, and my turning to the arts for a bit of pleasant writing. Shucks, I hope my American friends don't feel I am abandoning them. I must reassure them that I'll be back soon at the old whipping post.

I must explain why being rough and tough on US Embassy bullies, politicians and big business, I am unfailingly gentle with our artists.

Well, honkies, hacks and curmudgeons have uncommonly thick skins and can stand a lot of beating. They need to be feared and hated, to accomplish the job they want to do, which is to screw the Filipino people.

But artists are different. They spend so much of their lives and energy just to be loved and appreciated by their audience. They are only as good as their last performance, their productive life is short and financially unrewarding. What sustains them is a frail and fragile ego, a pride in their craft.

It is so easy to destroy their ego, and their lives. And I will not be party to it. If I cannot say something nice, I won't say it. These artists sacrifice too much of themselves to give us joy in this life. And that is a hell of a lot more than I can say of honkies, hacks and curmudgeons.

Last week we were again treated to an evening of ballet, this time featuring the choreographers and the dance corps, no prima ballerinas. And it was perfection.

Saint Exupery once wrote, "Perfection is reached not when there is nothing more to add, but when there is nothing more to take away." Perfection is simplicity, requiring no frills to bring it across.

- Perry Sevidal is quicksilver, the fastest dancer in the corps, who could bring more alegro, more humoresque to a dance than most.

- Melissa Cuachon is a revelation, a paragon of pulchritude on stage, whether adagio or allegro she projects an dream-like quality that is ethereal, heavenly.

- Ida Beltran is lyrical and gorgeous, specially when she performs an arabesque, lifting her leg behind her body, very high and very stretched.

- Nonoy Froilan, as usual in full command of his craft, is as often described here and abroad, ``elegant, versatile and eloquent.''

- Gina Katigbak always gives her roles an inner glow, a character, and she plays trippingly on her steps to give them freshness and spontaneity.

- Conrad Dy-Liacco, brilliant, dramatic, intense, dedicated, adds more facets to the role he plays.

- Sofia Zobel, who looks top-heavy, is always a delight to watch because she has such impressive presence on stage, a strength, grace, elegance and a feel for the comic and dramatic. By God, I like her. She makes up for all the implosion of office buildings, condominiums, narrow streets and traffic jams, the clutter and overcrowding, in Makati that her father Jaime is responsible for. **[Nota Bene, 2002: For this paragraph, Jaime Zobel sues me for libel, see Part 3 below]**

But the credits for the evening belong to the

choreographers: Alfred Rodrigues of Great Britain for his Variaciones Concertantes; Norman Walker for his Satan's Soliloquy; William Morgan for his Paquita; Tony Fabella for his Batuque; Paulie Koner (shades of Martha Graham!) for her Concertino; and Denisa Reyes for her Te Deum.

Religious themes deserve the highest artistic expression, and that is why I am most impressed with Walker's Satan's Soliloquy, and Denisa Reyes' Te Deum.

Satan's Soliloquy is a solo piece by Conrad Dy-Liacco, as Satan delivering his curse on mankind and God. You can't imagine the malignant malevolence reflected in the body contortions and rippling muscles of this great dancer, with all his intimations of the serpent in Eden, Christ hissing "Get thee behind me Satan!"; the fiery battle where angels fell, and nuclear mushrooms, and radiation raining upon the earth; and the twin abominations of our modern world -- International Communism and American Imperialism.

Te Deum is a vivid interpretation of one of the most beautiful and moving hymns of this earth, sung in times of war and peace, to affirm our faith... *Te deum laudamus; te Dominum confitemur. Te aeternum Patrem, omnis terra veneratur... Sanctus, sanctus, sanctus, Dominus Deus Sabaoth. Pleni sunt coeli et terra, majestatis gloriae tuae.*

We praise Thee, O God; we acknowledge thee to be the Lord. Thee, the Father everlasting, all the earth doth worship... Holy, holy, holy, Lord God of Hosts. Full are the heavens and the earth of the majesty of Thy glory!

From the anguished cry of Jesus, *"Eli, Eli, lama sabacthani? -- My God, my God, why hast thou forsaken me?"* to the joyous Resurrection and Transfiguration of our Lord!
November 7, 1989, Philippine Daily Inquirer

Part 2. Ruthless Ayala avarice, unmitigated greed

ONE has only to go to Makati during morning, noon and afternoon rush hours to see clogged traffic arteries bursting to the full. One has only to live and work in Makati to see the facilities for phones, water, electricity and sewage strained to excess -- the swirling dust, the noxious fumes; car horns, stereo blasts, noise pollution -- unsightly neonlights and a forest of TV antennas struggling to capture faint electronic signals ricocheting, spent and lost in the abyss of cliffs and precipices of tall buildings -- the heat radiating from asphalt and cement, the sweat and the dirt, the screams and the curses -- the rampant theft and drug abuse, carnapping and gun duels that plague a population driven to insanity by being compressed into so small an area. And a Tom Thumb of a mayor you cannot locate even with a microscope.

And you wonder what unmitigated greed, what ruthless merciless avarice would move the Zobels of Ayala y CIA to allow two more hotel complexes where there should be more green parks and parking places.

There are four large five-star hotels in Makati: Intercon, Peninsula, Manila Gardens, Mandarin. There will soon be two more: Shangri-La Hotel on Ayala corner Makati Ave. where Rizal Theater used to be; and the New World Hotel, on Pasay Road corner Makati Ave.

The two will be the highest and the largest: Shangri-La with 28 storeys and 600 rooms; the New World with 27 storeys and 550 rooms -- and together with them will blossom over a hundred additional shops and restaurants.

What complicates the traffic in Makati is the multitude of shopping malls and eating places. Every store and every restaurant brings with it at least a hundred cars a day on shopping trips. Movie houses require even more parking spaces.

We need more condominiums in the area to accommodate the hardy cliff-dwellers, denizens who dare to reside where their work place is within walking distance. Every condo needs only one car parking space, compared to 100 to every store, restaurant or movie house.

The Makati Developers Association headed by Conrad Leviste want precisely to build higher condo buildings to accommodate more of these cliff dwellers, and is bringing Ayala to court for restricting buildings only to eight floors.

Conrad argues that the more cliff dwellers in Makati, the less of a traffic problem, and the added sewage may be disposed of by more efficient sewage treatment facilities of building owners.

Ayala's restrictions were acceptable twenty years ago when land was only P350 per square meter in Legaspi and Salcedo Villages, but today, at P60,000 per square meter and astronomical construction costs, it is imperative to make more efficient land use by building higher condos.

What really sticks in the throat is the thought that the Zobels of Ayala do not follow their own restrictions, and allowed lackadaisical violations like that of

- Nauru Building at the corner of Buendia and Makati in front of DBP, which was allowed to build to 110 meters instead of being restricted to 90 meters as others are.
- Atrium Office Building in the Apartment Ridge Area on Makati Avenue near Bing Limcaco's Olympia Apartments.
- Insular Life Building on Ayala Avenue where they put up a grocery store on the ground floor where stores are usually forbidden.

Neither has the Ayala been giving adequate consideration to the open spaces, 30 percent of property, mandated by law. As a matter of fact the Ayala has been using and selling open spaces zoned by the Metro Manila Commission.

- The large area at the corner of Buendia and Ayala Avenue was sold by Ayala to China Bank, which in turn sold it to Rizal Commercial Bank (RCBC) which could not build on it because it is supposed to be open space.
- One Salcedo Place condominium on Alfaro Street near the Makati Sports Club is built on an area designated as a sports field or open space, where Ayala destroyed large ancient acacia trees without the required permit from the authorities.

Swapang! *Tuso*! *Switik*! Not content trying to perpetuate our colonial mentality by naming their villages Magallanes instead of Lapu-Lapu; Forbes instead of Quezon; Urdaneta, Dasmariñas, Salcedo, Legaspi, instead of Rizal, Bonifacio, Aguinaldo, Luna --

Not content with spurning our noble bloodlines, and laundering their genes among the crude peasants of rural Spain -- not content accumulating enormous wealth in our poor country, more than they can spend in a hundred lifetimes, while we poor Flips live a marginal existence at the edge of starvation --

Not content inflicting upon us Cesar Buenaventura, Shell and the Council of Trent -- the Ayalas heap upon us in Makati their abominable greed and avarice.

February 3, 1990, Philippine Daily Inquirer

Part 3. Thanks, Jaime Zobel, you made my day!

DON'T worry, dear readers, about the P240 million libel suit filed against me by Don Jaime Zobel de Ayala. I have been sued before, writing on your behalf -- for P10 million each by Juan Ponce Enrile, Ricardo Romulo and Christian Monsod -- and I am still around to serve you.

Big lawyers offered to defend me free of charge, and all of them tell me that of all the libel cases filed against me, Zobel's case is the weakest, and may not even reach the courts.

This is because, according to them, the two alleged libelous articles, entitled "Full of the heavens and the earth (PDI, Nov.7,1989)"' and "Avarice, unmitigated greed in Makati (PDI, Feb.3,1990)"' deal with a subject that of prime PUBLIC INTEREST, and a person who is undoubtedly a PUBLIC FIGURE.

Certainly the implosion of buildings, narrow streets and traffic jams in the Makati Commercial Center, compounded by the two hotel complexes being built, is of public interest to residents and those who work in Makati, who daily suffer the aggravations of being trapped inside a snake pit of sweat, dust, a cacophony of honking horns and inextricable traffic jams.

Certainly the head of the corporation responsible for the planning and layout of this commercial area, one of the biggest companies in the Philippines, is a public figure subject to legitimate comment and criticism. With easier access than I have to television, radio and print media (even in my own column), Jaime has all the facilities to answer any criticisms I direct against him.

Friends fear that "as in many suits filed by the rich against the poor, fixers and shysters may influence fiscals, judges and justices to render an unjust decision." Please not to worry, we have every confidence on the integrity of our judicial system.

Whatever shenanigans (highly unlikely) may be contemplated, cannot be done under the full glare of publicity. No judge will risk his reputation and career rendering a patently unjust and unfair judgment when there are reporters, lawyers and columnists watching the proceedings.

Not only do I have offers of legal assistance, but there are witnesses ready to testify on the ethics and practices of the Ayalas.   Horror stories of landgrabbing and other instances of "avarice and unmitigated greed" will be told by many, including Rene Knecht, a poor Spanish widow., and a *masahista* at the Makati Sports.

Jaime Zobel and I have always been civil to each other because although I criticize him, I am an unabashed fan of his daughter, ballet dancer Sofia, and his wife Bea, an involved do-gooder.   We often meet at concerts at the CCP, and always have a few minutes of humorous bantering.

Former Speaker Pepito Laurel told me that Jaime must be a good friend of mine, because he honors me with the biggest libel suit (bigger than Danding Cojuangco's P100 million suit against the Bulletin) in the history of Philippine jurisprudence, "As if you are not big enough," he said, "Jaime wants to make you even bigger."

Nestor Mata says I should demand to be sued for P2 billion.

Joan Orendain says "The very fact that Jaime sues you for P240 million is incontrovertible proof of his avarice.   He flatters you in the process."

The family of the poor girl Rosario, who died an excruciating death because of a broken vibrator inserted by a foreigner into her vagina, was awarded damages of only P30,000.

Jaime really made my day.   Here is proof of the impact of our Inquirer with its audited circulation almost equal to Bulletin, and with three times the Bulletin's circulation in the provinces.

Jaime made my day by implying that I am the best read and most influential columnist in the country, that my mighty pen can, in three paragraphs, do P240 million worth of damage to his peace of mind.   That is 80,000 times more damage to Jaime than the foreigner's broken vibrator did to poor dead Rosario.

It has been rumored that his lawyer, a modern version of the famous Vicente Francisco, demanded and got an acceptance fee of P5 million to prosecute this case.

By God, Jaime, for a lot less than that amount, you can

help Mrs. Bernardita G. de Jesus, Lot 6 Block 31, Bonita Homes, Concepcion, Marikina.

Her youngest child, aged one and a half years, is in need of cardiac surgery. She has a congenital heart defect called "tetralogy of fallot" that is potentially fatal if not corrected.

Deborah Heart & Lung Center in New Jersey USA is willing to provide all medical and surgical care free of charge, if Mrs. de Jesus can bring the baby there at the own expense. She needs travel and personal expenses.

Help them, Jaime Zobel, and I promise that for such act of charity, I will sing you praises to high heaven that will give you the Big O.

March 11, 1990, Philippine Daily Inquirerl

Part 4. Lifestyles of the filthy rich and infamous

JAIME ZOBEL made my day by alleging that three paragraphs I wrote has caused him P240 million worth of damages. That is 80,000 times the P30,000 damages awarded little Rosario who died an excruciating death from a broken vibrator inserted into her vagina by a foreign pedophile. I guess the rich are entitled to more sympathy than the poor.

Jaime should be further pained to note that the Housing and Land Use Regulatory Board (HLURB) has supported my position by restraining Ayala from enforcing the deed restrictions for Salcedo and Legaspi Villages. Ayala has been imposing restrictions on others which it is not imposing on itself. For all legal purposes, Ayala's restrictions are, for the moment, considered canceled.

The HLURB also restrained Ayala from pursuing the construction of their project, One Salcedo Place, which is presently being built on an area intended for open space.

But a *Bulletin* news item said otherwise: that the court stopped work on Makati condos being restricted by Ayala rules, when actually such rules were suspended by the court. The rich can manipulate the truth.

I hope a group of Makati citizens can secure a court injunction against the two hotel complexes being built in the Makati Commercial Center, on the grounds that such will put a strain on existing facilities for utilities and also lead to further traffic congestion.

We are glad to note indeed that the power of old oligarchs to influence officialdom and the courts is waning, even as more aggressive entrepreneurs like Henry Sy, John Gokongwei and Lucio Tan are fast overtaking them in wealth.

History shows that human institutions, ranging from royal dynasties to families born to wealth and power, inevitably fade away with time. This is attributable to the tendency of families to keep the power and wealth to themselves by incest and inbreeding.

This is turn brings out recessive traits of insanity, idiocy and congenital diseases that lead to retardation and inevitable oblivion.

The imperial families of Egypt, Rome and China are no more, decimated by internecine warfare and fratricide. The royal families of Spain are subject to insanity and those of Russia to hemophilia. The Rothchilds, Hapsburgs, and de Medicis have had more than their share of idiots, crazies and faggots.

The only human institution that is immune from all these abominations is the Catholic Church, which lasted for 2,000 years, because its wellsprings are constantly replenished by new blood. Celibacy is the reason for its survival.

Be glad, dear readers, that you are not filthy rich. It's worse than being poor. You may discover for instance that your great great grandmother was an adulteress and your great grandmother married her half-brother, an act of incest that plants the seed of insanity into your blood.

Instant and infinite gratification of your sexual appetites may satiate and dull your senses, driving you to unnatural and aberrant behavior with your own sex.

If you are prone to athletics, you can buy a whole football team or even two basketball teams to play with.

If you are like Howard Hughes, you'd make your most important business deals inside a public toilet, re-invent the brassiere and make movies so you can seduce the leading lady, then end your days as a super-hypochondriac, cannot stand being with people without being thoroughly disinfected, and cared for by religious fanatics expecting to inherit your fortune.

If you are like Barbara Hutton, you'd be marrying every gigolo and fortune hunter in sight, beaten up by sadists, cheated by every con-man and scam artist, and end up a lonely, loveless witch.

If you are like Caligula, you will make love to your own sister, murder your own mother, promote your horse to a high government position, end up being a raving maniac and murdered by your own security guards.

If you are like Imelda Marcos, you will procure 3,000 shoes you wear only once, loot the nation of its resources and take the food out of your own people's mouths, get accused of fraud and robbery, face a prison term, sing out of tune and get fat.

If you are like a Malacañang crony, with a squint acquired from a lifetime habit of peering through darkened windows preparatory to an act of thievery, your nose will grow like Pinocchio's and try to say hello to your chin over a protesting mouth deprived of its living space and twisted to one side. Like The Picture of Dorian Gray, this is the price of unmitigated villainy and treason in the service of a foreign power.

Dear readers, to be moderately wealthy and comfortable is to be desired. But to be filthy rich beyond all reason and beyond all bounds, is worse than being poor. It is hell on earth.

March 21, 1990, Philippine Daily Inquirer

[Nota Bene, 2002. Subsequently Jaime Zobel called me up to say that he would rather be my friend than my enemy. He signed a letter of desistance, and settled out of court with my promise not to write about him for the next three years.]

Part 5. Of Jaime, Jobo, JoeCon and Jerks

JAIME ZOBEL and I have finally made peace. Through a common friend, a luncheon meeting was arranged and we talked matters over. I told him that it was not my intention to hurt him as I do admire his wife Bea and his daughter Sofia.

Jaime is a person with two distinct characters -- one as an artist and the other as a businessman. As an artist, he is to be admired. As a businessman, Jaime Zobel must be prepared to be criticized on the actuations of his corporation.

I agreed to address the issues of Makati Commercial without bias or prejudice, as long as we keep our lines open and communicate when necessary.

On his part, he said he would withdraw his P240 million libel suit against me, which flattered me no end, and promised to keep in touch. In parting Jaime gave me two books, one on the paintings of Fernando Zobel and a Folio of his own photos called The Sea.

I always did like artists, they give so much of themselves to give joy to others, and get so little in return. In my book, artists are on a higher stage of evolution than those creeps -- big businessmen, politicians and CIA bums.

I am talking about real artists, not those fornicating little brats on screen and TV, who can't act beyond huffing, puffing, peeling, and singing like cats on a hot tin roof.

Well, Jaime is a sensitive artist and a patron of the arts. And a real philanthropist. I did hear from my editor (which Jaime confirmed) that he saw Mr. Bernardita de Jesus, whose child did go to the USA and died on the operating table. He helped the family anyway, God bless him.

The trouble is that aside being an artist, Jaime is also a businessman. And as such he is in a free fire zone. I mean, everyone who gets stuck in Makati traffic automatically makes a mental note of someday strangling Jaime.

So we have to draw a fine line between Jaime the artist and Jaime the businessman.

Jaime and I agreed on the ground rules. When I raise an issue of public concern, like what is being built in Makati Commercial Center, I would be grateful for a reaction from him or his company publicly or privately.

I want an open honorable battle, a free and unlimited debate, a real Socratic Dialogue. No stonewalling on Ayala's part. And no more personal insults from me.

That's why I'm disappointed with Jobo. When I was in the Cabinet, I consulted him, even asked him to write a column with me on the front page of the old Manila Times. Same with those jerks Ting Jayme, Geny Lopez, and Bernie Villegas.

They have no call to avoid me as if they had something to hide, or stonewall the issues by silence, exhibiting an insensitivity as thick as an elephant's ass. They just do not care what anybody else thinks.

Same with JoeCon the Misconception. We were together for so long in the Philippine Chamber of Industries, along with Salvador Araneta, his father-in-law who always treated me like a son.

I want to remind JoeCon that when I was in the Cabinet as Chairman of the National Economic Council, I had wide powers in the adjustment of tariff rates -- just I and President Macapagal.

JoeCon and Don Salvador came to my office, even without appointment, and when their request was in the national interest, I complied, even against the interest of my family firm.

Upon their request, I raised the tariff rates on soya bean oil -- which they manufactured and which my family firm imported. I raised the rates on flour and lowered the rates on wheat, and gave birth to the flour industry. I raised the rates on air conditioners, refrigerators and appliances, and lowered the rates on black iron sheets, and gave birth to the appliance industry.

Damn it, the Concepcions owe me their billions.

All I ask JoeCon today is to do for the nation what I did for the Concepcions... only two things:

- Integrate the steel industry. I don't care if Concepcion uses iron sheets and tin plates made from billets imported by National Steel -- it simply is not logical that we export iron ore at $25 per ton and import it back as billets at $250 per ton. Ongpin technocrats seized the industry by force to prevent real industrialization, and used it as a milking cow. While Lopez, Soriano, Emilio Yap, Lucio Tan got their companies back, JoeCon and the Ongpin boys want Jacinto to go to court, so that the steel integration may be delayed for ten years more!

- Put the Petrochemical Industry out of the control of Shell, out of the monopoly of foreigners, and back to Bataan where it belongs. Foreign investors are not entitled to discounts on our debt papers, loans by our institutions and from our ADB allocations.

- I don't expect to win all my battles, but I am entitled to be

listened to, and given due consideration, especially by JoeCon who seems deaf and dumb.
June 12, 1998, Philippine Daily Inquirer

Part 6. Jaime Zobel de Zobel, not de Ayala

My uncle, historian Carlos Quirino, came to me one day with two manuscripts in his hand, "I have here two books that will forever be unpublished because it tells the unvarnished truth about two powerful families. It has been my practice when I write a book about anyone, not to depend on family sources, but to try to solicit more interesting facts from family friends and associates, especially those with old letters from the past. One such letter came from Allan Mihalle, a great great grandnephew of Dr. John Burke, the doctor who attended Doña Margarita Roxas de Ayala on her death bed, and inadvertently heard her death bed confession. The letter was in German and sent by Dr. Burke to his brother and sisters, whose descendant is Allan. The letter was translated and thereby hangs a tale."

Doña Margarita Roxas de Ayala is the daughter of Don Domingo Roxas of the family which owned vast lands in Barrio San Pedro Makati – the source of the Ayala-Zobel fortune. She married Don Antonio Ayala and bore two daughters: Carmen and Trinidad. Carmen married her first cousin Pedro Pablo Roxas for who she bore a daughter Margarita who married Eduardo Soriano and bore a son Andres, the fabled Don Andres Soriano of San Miguel Brewery.

The younger daughter of Doña Margarita, Trinidad Ayala married Jacobo Zobel, Hijo, and bore among others Enrique, grandfather of Enriquito "EZ" Zobel who sold his San Miguel stocks to Danding Cojuangco; and Jaime Zobel de Ayala, who now owns Ayala y CIA.

Doña Margarita is the greatest philanthropist the Philippines has even known, having donated La Concordia College, La Consolacion College and various real estates all over to country to charity. One always wondered why she was so generous. Perhaps she was currying favor with God for some dark and secret reason.

The letter of Dr. John Burke, told the story with a snicker, "I must make ye laugh... after the birth of Carmen,

Doña Margarita separated from her husband and went from him to the province, and there met old (Jacobo) Zobel and they fell in love with each other. Soon after, her husband Don Antonio, hearing this, (reconciled with her). A few months later Trinidad was born. Don Antonio and Doña Margarita lived on (friendly) terms. I attended her during her last sickness.

"(While dying) she called Trinidad who was then flirting with the young Zobel, and Don Antonio her husband, and with Padre Bertran as witness, made Trinidad swear on a crucifix that she'd never marry Zobel, and made Antonio swear he'd never permit the match. Doña Margarita died and left a paper confessing to Don Antonio (that) Trinidad was the daughter of Old (Jacobo) Zobel, and (asking him) never to permit a marriage between them (her and her half brother).

"Secret relations commenced (between Trinidad and her half brother young Zobel, 10 years her senior). Old Ayala swore he'd never permit the match. (Then) he fell sick with *disgusto* (a mild heart attack), and after six weeks, almost dying and out of his mind, he consented (in delirium to the marriage).

"They were married, and on their return from the church, he recovered and learned what had happened. (He) continued dying, in his delirium to the hour of his death. I was present (at all times) by his bedside at his dying moment. It turns out that Trinidad is married to her brother....."

Most Spaniards will endure anything except being cuckolded (*pendejo* is the pejorative word). He and his wife forbade Trinidad from marrying young Zobel, but never told her why. Not knowing the secret, and she married her own half brother, Jacobo Zobel, Hijo. She never had a drop of Don Antonio Ayala's blood. Therefore her descendants should not assume the family name Zobel de Ayala, both her father and husband being surnamed Zobel. The desacendants should rightly be called Zobel de Zobel.

July 22, 2002, unpublished

ooooo

CHAPTER 6. Characters in my life

Part 1. Claude Wilson, *maski dios kumukupas rin*

CLAUDE WILSON, bless his soul, is no longer with us, but I cherish the memory of our battles together in the Jaycees and in the Chamber of Industries and our trips as fellow travelers.

An American GI who settled here and married a Filipina, Isabel Caro, he and I were partners in the Claude Wilson Corporation (now Business Machines Corporation) and in the Philippine Sewing Machine Corp. We set up a foundry to manufacture for the first time a sewing machine in the Philippines, got entangled in a fight with Singer Sewing Machine Co. who insisted that Filipinos should not manufacture here, but should continue to import from Singer.

We won the argument but lost the business, because the Central Bank gave Singer a hefty dollar allocation for machinery and raw materials, and left us, the pioneers to wither on the vine because we did not have "market acceptability." Dung.

Because of the colonial mentality of our officials, the American multinationals continue to own us body and soul.

Traveling together, planing home with some Jaycee friends, Claude Wilson turned to me: "Larry, if you have any dutiable articles, entrust them to me. I'll get them through customs."

"No thanks, Claudio, I can manage," I answered.

I followed him through the customs area, when I heard this customs man say ever so sweetly, "Welcome home, Mr. Wilson. No, no, not necessary to open your bags. Please walk right through."

Since I was in his company I followed him, but the customs man shoved me back roughly, raising his voice, *"Hintay ka muna, pare, hindi pa ako tapos sa iyo,"* and pointing to my luggage, he demanded, *"Buksan mo!"*

Now, I am sure that if the Concavity and Convexity of their faces were confronted by the same situation, they would have called Claude Wilson to come back and help them.

But not me. Not Henares the nationalist. I was

delighted at the opportunity to wave the flag.

"WHAT!!" I screamed at the top of my voice, "You mean to say, you son of a whore, that Americans have privileges in this country that is denied to fellow Filipinos??"

Oh my countrymen, you should have seen the expression on the face of that arrogant pro-American jackass as people all around focused their attention on us.

There was surprise, consternation, panic, a kind of whimpering, asinine look of despair, as I shouted, "Where is the Airport Customs Commissioner? I want to complain against this son of a female dog. I will not open my luggage unless the luggage of the American is also inspected. I refuse to be treated like dung in my own country."

It was delightful, it was delicious, I was savoring it to the full, when Claude Wilson sidled back to me and whispered, "Larry, for God's sake, I'll pay for your duties, but please, please shut up already."

But I was enjoying myself too much to pay attention to Claude, "Sorry, Claudio, this is a matter of principle. Besides, it is too late, that's Commissioner Salvador Mascardo approaching."

I was in my early thirties, sexy and slim at 125 lbs., with a complete set of wavy hair and I must have looked like a jerk to Badong Mascardo. With dagger looks at the pro-American jackass, he asked both Claude Wilson and me to open our bags.

Anak ng kalabaw, I became sorry I started all the ruckus, because when they opened Claude Wilson's baggages, they found all the highly dutiable articles extant -- transistor radios, liquor, cigarets, watches, jewelry.

Claude Wilson was sweating, as I apologized, "Jimminy krauts, Claudio, I am sorry, I didn't know you were a smuggler on such a large scale."

Claude stared at me, and laughed and laughed till I thought he had gone crazy, "Smuggler, my foot, those articles belong to our fellow Jaycees, our fellow passengers! They entrusted them to me."

I looked back and saw the rest of our fellow Jaycees staring at me. If looks could kill, I would have dropped dead right then and there. And a year would pass before any of them would talk to me again.

The Jaycee gang broke up eventually, but Claude and I kept in touch as neighbors in Dasmariñas Village, reminiscing about old times when we were business partners and I was vice-president of his companies.

He was a thespian with the looks of William Holden in the Manila Theater Guild, while I was in charge of the lights and sound. He sadly recounted a movie role he played as an American father to Hilda Koronel *hanggang pier lamang.* In a scene where he came back old and ugly, his daughter Hilda was moved to exclaim, "*Maski dios, kumukupas rin.* Even a god shrivels."

In an American TV documentary, Claude was pictured in a party in his house, surrounded by fellow Americans awash with prosperity, playing the piano and singing, "Happy Days Are Here Again." while scenes of poverty and degradation among Filipinos during martial law were maliciously intercut with his bacchanalia.

Claude was mad, "Those bastards asked me to sing that song so they can make a monkey out of me."

Claude Wilson died before the February Revolution, and with him died that part of my life when I genuinely liked Americans.

I tell this story to show that this battle of mine against our Colonial Mentality started long ago, and will never be finished until every Filipino (including Sostenes Campillo, Uncle Tom Monsod, Small Dick Romulo, Alopecic Misogamic Gynander Villegas) and every American too, learns to respect Filipinos, as Claude Wilson did.

If this means having to show that bossy Americans are no better than we are, that they are just ordinary, run-of-the-mill garden-variety human beings with 25 feet of intestines, full of shit like all the rest of us -- if it means having to slay the American Father Image, then so be it.

There are many things good about the Americans, and not all multinationals are bad, but we shall leave the trumpeting to their hired hacks and paid pipers.

This column will speak for the Filipino.

December 16, 1987, Philippine Daily Inquirer

Part 2. Ramon Diaz lets out a primal scream; Ninoy owes me P50

NINOY AQUINO and I were fond of categorizing people into Screamers, Smilers and Frowners.

Nationalists, we observed, are screamers by nature. Sensitive about any intrusions on national sovereignty or national interest, they scream at the least provocation. Ding Lichauco is a screamer.

American and their agents are frowners. *Iniipon ang galit.* They never get mad, they just get even. The facilities of NBI, NICA and CIS are at their disposal. Jimmy Ongpin and Phil Kaplan are frowners.

Then the smilers, the nice guys, the salt of the earth. Neither nationalists nor colonials, they thrive because they are acceptable to a fractious polarized society. PCGG Chairman Ramon Diaz and Comelec Chairman Ramon Felipe are smilers.

It is easy to get the Screamers mad. They are highly emotional because they are fighting against the status quo, and only charged emotions can move people to effect change. One has only to read Patrick Henry and Samuel Adams (of the American Revolution), and Voltaire and Jean Jacques Rousseau (of the French Revolution) to realize how necessary this is. I am a screamer.

It is almost impossible to get the Frowners mad. They are defending the status quo. Any quarrel will imperil what advantage they already have. Therefore they counsel prudence, sobriety, calmness and dispassion in order to defuse any danger. The boring speeches of Jimmy Ongpin, Christian Monsod and Bernie Villegas, are meant to mesmerize their audience to inaction. No matter how much they are challenged or provoked, or insulted, they will not respond in kind. When pushed to the limit, they usually suffer a nervous breakdown.

Smilers are there to create goodwill, to keep everyone happy. In a way, they help preserve the status quo, so the screamers are not at all happy about them.

Ninoy said that the screamers are emotionally the healthiest because they get rid of their frustrations fast, but they are irritating because they are always angry. Like me.

The frowners, he said, because of the tremendous pressure of their bottled-up anger, are potential patients of the insane asylum. Jimmy Ongpin is feeling the pressure; he snarls all the time and calls his tormentors garbage. It takes just a little more to push him over the edge **[Note 2002: Eventually Jimmy committed suicide]**

But the smilers are the ones most human; it takes a long while to get them mad. But when they do, they let out a primal scream, a cry of pain, get rid of the bile in their system, and let be bygones be bygones. Afterwards, they are as happy and pleasant as they ever were.

Ninoy bet me P50.00 that I will never succeed in getting the goat of Ramon Diaz and Ramon Felipe, their reservoir of goodwill seemed inexhaustible. For twenty years I never succeeded, till I started to write a daily column.

Well, fifty bucks is fifty bucks, and I sure hate to think that I owe that much to a National Hero. I must earn it back somehow.

And I did. I made both Ramons cry in pain, mad enough to say words so alien to their upbringing as pillars of Ateneo's Sodality of Our Lady. Ninoy now owes me P50.00, and I wonder if I should send the bill to Kris.

Comelec Chairman Ramon Felipe was first on the agenda. Let's face it, Mon is so pleasant, so accommodating, so full of the milk of human kindness, it was almost a sacrilege to ruffle his feathers.

Our first quarrel was about Mike Lorza's Abacus System of voter's registration and vote tabulation that made use of IBM compatibles. Namfrel's Christian Monsod arrogantly dismissed Lorza, then sent Gus Lagman to contact Allen Weinstein of the Center of Democracy, who was peddling a mainframe system involving millions of dollars.

In spite of warnings that Allen Weinstein may be a CIA agent intent on corrupting our electoral processes, Christian invited Weinstein to the Philippines and even brought him to Malacanang. All the time, he told Mike Lorza that he is even worth talking to.

When Christian got Weinstein to Ramon Felipe of the Comelec, and Felipe began to make pro-American noises, it was the time for me to cry Ouch. I am a screamer after all.

I wrote a series of articles about Ramon Felipe --- on the third one, he let out a primal scream. He called me all sorts of names, but in the end, his good humor prevailed,

Weinstein was scuttled and Mike Lorza's system is getting a try-out in Muntinlupa.

Instead of dismantling the crony power structure, PCGG has been using Piedra to control Orient, UCPB to control San Miguel, *ad nauseum.*   As PCGG chairman, Ramon Diaz had to take the flak. I wrote a funny piece about a nosy American who kept calling him "Raymund THE Ass". On San Miguel we had an honest difference of opinion. Aside from all the logical arguments, I brought in a device called "historical and literary allusion", a weapon of a combative intellect.

First, I saw the battle as one between Michael the Archangel and Lucifer. Second, I brought in Dr. Fu Manchu and the Dragon Lady on the side of Lucifer. Third, I saw Ramon as Brutus guilty of Caesar's death, assisted by two Brides of Frankenstein *(Et tu, Bruja).*   Lastly, he became Hitler, Napoleon and Genghis Khan with the combined power of Danding Cojuangco, Kokoy Romualdez, and the cronies.

Ramon Diaz, the nice guy and smiler, finally let out a primal scream:

"All the time you made people believe you are a nationalist and hater of Americans ... until you sold your soul to one. You have the gall to heap insults, ridicule and calumnies on me. You picked on me to earn your spurs under your new boss. I am sure you will be editor soon. No amount of calumnies, insults, misrepresentations, exaggerations, lies and ridicule will deter me from doing what I think is right."

Neither San Miguel nor any one connected with Andy is taking over the Inquirer, believe me, Mon. The battle is over and you have won. Having gotten rid of your bile, you can smile again.

Now Kris, pay up Ninoy's fifty bucks.

May 20, 1987, Philippine Daily Inquirer

Part 3. Jojo, you'd hate being tall like Vic Lim

ONCE upon a time, there was a fellow from China called Lim. His full name was Lim Ahong, or Limahong, and he mounted an expedition from China to the Philippines. After months at sea without the company of women, he landed in Lingayen, Pangasinan, and the first thing he did was to chase a girl up a coconut tree. Poor girl, to her dying day she never knew the real culprit, whether Lim Ahong ... or the coconut tree.

Generations later, looking at his descendant, Victor A. Lim, 6 feet on his stockinged feet, we are inclined to believe... by God, it was the coconut tree!

Jojo Binay, we write to let you know that you are better off being a little runt than a 6 footer like Victor Lim. Really.

To be a giant among small people is terrible. Poor Vic, all the time he has to dodge low doorways and bump his head getting into small cars. He stands out in any crowd, cannot maintain enough anonymity to do what comes naturally to a full-blooded male; he's been caught so many times by his wife, he even thought of retiring to a monastery.

He stoops, he crouches, he cowers, to keep from being noticed, all in vain. He can not even pick his nose without making an public spectacle out of it.

In Ateneo high school, as Victor Lim walked down the corridor, all eyes would focus on him. At such a moment, Ramon M. Osmeña and myself, both about 5"6', would sidle up and walk beside him, Moning on the left and I on the right.

Then I would say to Moning, "Hi, left ball!" and Moning would answer back, "Hi, right ball!" and then both us would look up at Vic and laugh, as everybody did, because Vic really looked like a monumental phallic symbol.

To be tall and thin, as Vic is, is to have a high center of gravity and precarious sense of balance. That is why Vic walks like one of those circus performers balancing a ball and a pole on his forehead --- you know, his hips swivel, his arms swing out, his legs move forward and sideways in a desperate effort to keep his head perched on his neck from falling on its face.

Vic is a genius, a talented writer and effective speaker, a terrific leader of men who cares enough about his friends to recommend them for a job or introduce them to the right people or to raise campaign funds for them.

When we were kids, he was always the head of the gang. I always thought he would be president someday, and he probably would have been, had God not made him such a beanpole, so embarrassingly conspicuous that he spent most of his life trying to keep from being noticed.

Believe me, Jojo, you are lucky to be a runt.

Go to Fort Santiago, Jojo, and measure Jose Rizal's wardrobe, and you will see that he was as small as you are. Here was a genius: doctor of medicine, ophthalmologist, surgeon, biologist, engineer, historian, novelist, poet, painter, sculptor, swordsman, boxer, lover, linguist, nationalist, citizen of the world, martyr, and national hero -- the greatest the Malay race ever produced, and he was a runt like you.

Then there was the Little Corporal Napoleon Bonaparte who challenged the crowned heads of Europe, and intentionally or not, spread the ideals of the French Revolution --- liberty, equality, fraternity --- the Rights of Man and the Constitution, the metric system, Roman Law, universal education, nationalism and democracy. He also was a runt like you; as are Henri de Toulouse Lautrec, Tom Thumb, and Leonie Perez.

Jojo, being a conspicuous beanpole like Vic Lim is likely to land you into the role of a stalking horse and a scapegoat. A stalking horse is led forward to distract, so its master stalking behind may be able to take a good shot at the quarry; a stalking horse is a person put forward to mislead. A scapegoat is one chosen to suffer the sins of others.

PCCI president Vic Lim was the stalking horse and scapegoat of the Banker's Association and the Makati Business Club, who used him to advance their aim to give the Americans a lease on the bases after 1992, and to surrender Filipino interests to the IMF and foreign bankers.

Thus did the bankers and "monsters of greed" make a jackass out of Victor, just because he was born conspicuous. And now that he has served his purpose and is no longer of any use to them, Vic is relegated to the background, no longer the president of PCCI.

Better to be short and small and mayor of Makati, Jojo, all you have to contend with is Councilor Brilliantes, and his pubic relations man Adi Sison.

That is certainly less humiliating than chasing a girl up a coconut tree, and winding up to be a horse, a goat and a jackass.
January 19, 1987, Philippine Daily Inquirer

Part 4. Nikki Coseteng and nemesis Maganto
ANNA Dominique "Nikki" Coseteng cannot complain to

God Almighty, who lavished on her (1) exquisite beauty in translucent alabaster, (2) twice the brains of Platt, Reagan and Bush combined, (3) more wealth then she can spend in ten lifetimes.

Not satisfied with just beauty, brains, and wealth, Nikki demanded and got from God (4) a sense of nationalism, and (5) a copious source of righteous indignation to go with it.

With these five attributes, Nikki offered her services to the nation and was elected congresswoman of the third district of Quezon City.

As a nationalist she finds herself in direct collision with Bernie Villegas' CRC, Small Dick Romulo's MBC and Christian Monsod's BBC, clerico-fascists who are Filipino scalawags to the American carpetbagger; lame-brain lap dogs in the army and the police determined to butcher Filipinos opposed to foreign monopolies and American bases; and of course, the white trash neanderthals in the US and Australian embassies.

The CIA in particular is determined to attribute to Nikki Coseteng the awesome powers of a sex goddess, spreading delicious rumors of her love conquests from Senator Butz Aquino to Secretary Eddie Ramos, complete with lurid details worthy of Harold Robbins.

The rumor mongering CIA Rat Patrol has it that Nikki is already seven months pregnant. If she is, she is probably about to give birth to a tadpole, because she is as slim and sexy as Vilma Santos.

But the man chosen to be Nikki's nemesis by the Embassy's super spooks -- Cols. Denny Lane and Stephen Perry, as well as CIA chief Billygoat Lofgren -- is Lt. Col. Romeo Maganto, a policeman with the same level of intelligence and the same miasmic brain frontally lobotomized as most neanderthals have.

Romeo Maganto has been lionized in local movies as a Filipino Dirty Harry ("Go ahead punk, make my day!"), or Rambo ("I am your worst nightmare" which Sylvester Stallone masticates and spits out as "Myr wrst nghtmr").

Every lawyer knows that Dirty Harry and Rambo who are the heroes of Col. Maganto and President Reagan, are fascists who do not believe in habeas corpus, due process, the rule of law and democratic safeguards against official abuse. According to our informant, Lt. Col. Romeo Maganto is depicted as an avenging angel, the scourge of Communist Sparrow units.

In truth however, Maganto and his police have been accused of concentrating their ire on unarmed civilians who could not fight back, such as priests, nuns, human rights lawyers and students pasting placards on walls.

On June 24, 1988, Rep. Nikki Coseteng attended an affair in the Pope Pius XII Center, wherein a student, Hilario Bustamante Jr., known as JunJun, recounted how he and another student were pasting no-nukes and anti-bases posters on Taft Avenue when they were arrested by Maganto's minions.

JunJun claimed that both of them were horribly tortured, that his friend was hacked to death, his head almost completely severed from his body. JunJun escaped death by pretending to be dead, but his nape bore deep scars that extended across his back.

This diabolically cruel murder is the standard operating procedure of CIA-trained rightist death squads in El Salvador which assassinated Archbishop Romero and 10,000 workers, students, priests and nuns in 1980, just because they oppose American policies and belong to a race inferior to the Anglo-Saxons.

This affair in the Pope Pius XII Center was attended by QC councilor and ex chairman of the UP Student Council, Francis Pangilinan, film director Ishmael Bernal, Sister Pat Lardizabal, Reynaldo Lesaca and Redento. Nikki left early and saw no "mock trial" condemning Col. Maganto for murder.

The dinosaur became extinct because it took three hours for any nerve signal to travel through its nervous system from tail to brain. This delayed response to the presence of immediate danger spelled its doom.

It is symptomatic of pro-American jackasses that it took a full 28 days (from the June 24 affair to July 22) for the nerve signal to travel from their sphincter ani to their cerebral cortex, prompting them after a delayed reaction, to file charges of "illegal assembly" against Nikki Coseteng and the human rights activists.

That is why it is possible to predict with certainty that the CIA and their minions will soon be consigned to the

dustbin of history.
August 6, 1988, Philippine Daily Inquirer

Part 5. Singlaub setting up rightist Death Squads?

Is ex-CIA General John K. Singlaub trying to set up Death Squads among the Military and the Police?

U.S. Embassy, military, and Malacañang sources are beginning to piece together information indicating that Singlaub is talking right wing extremists into taking matters into their own hands "if the government persists in being wishy-washy about the Communists." This includes financing right-wing death squads in the military and the police to assassinate known "leftists, priests associated with Liberation Theology, and so-called nationalists," similar to what happened in El Salvador in 1980.

These sources revealed that somewhere in Makati was held on January 26, a meeting of rightist extremists headed by NICA chief Luis Villareal, ex-Senator Eva Estrada Kalaw, Chinese businessmen associated with the Taiwanese Kuomintang, Ramboys, Marcos loyalists, and some members of the Opus Dei. In this meeting Singlaub stressed the "necessity of self-protection" among big businessmen and financiers. The "self-protection" of El Salvador right-wingers consisted of financing right-wing death squads in the police and the military acting unofficially as hired killers. This led to the assassination of 9,000 people in El Salvador, including Archbishop Oscar Romero while saying mass in April 1980, and four American women --- three Maryknoll nuns and a Catholic lay worker --- on a dirt road in December 1980.

The Embassy source, who does not want to be identified, said that "Singlaub is operating here without official sanction from the U.S. State Department. He is strictly on his own. We do know his connection with Colonel Oliver North who was fired in Washington for the Iran/Contra Scam, and we do not discount the possibility that he is here on covert CIA business. We are keeping an eye on him."

Military sources say they are worried that Singlaub is talking to "right wingers in the military. big landowners and the Opus Dei, the same kind of people constituting the death squad financiers in El Salvador."

A high-up source in Malacañang admitted that

"Singlaub has been pestering the government for a permit to look for treasure. No wants to have the responsibility of getting involved in something ridiculous and absurd that may turn out to be a sting operation on the Moonies and the Taiwanese financiers, or a cover for some dark conspiracy. He also wants to have a security detail from the military, which we cannot give because according to law, no private individual may be so accorded." Some other informant said Singlaub got the necessary permit from Minister Jaime Ongpin.

The Malacañang informant also revealed that Singlaub is being "watched by intelligence agents, other than those of NICA (National Intelligence Coordinating Agency, the equivalent of the American CIA), the reason being that even during Martial Law and in the United States, NICA chief Luis Villareal and General Singlaub have been chummy long-time friends, fellow members of the anti-communist anti-nationalist clique."

The Malacañang source also said that Marcos Loyalists are going out of their way to meet with Singlaub "as part of the psywar being waged against the Aquino Administration, leading people to believe that the CIA and the Americans are supporting the Marcos oppositionists."

Other sources, mostly American businessmen, say that "Singlaub is nutty as a fruitcake, digging holes out in the boondocks and hiring an American diver named Allen to dive offshore out there in Batangas near Calatagan, when everybody knows there is no such thing as Yamashita's treasure. That sonamabitch is up to no good, but he will not succeed because the Filipinos are the biggest blabbermouths in the world. And everyone will know what he will do before he even does it."

Another informant said that Singlaub is really digging for treasure, "he reason Singlaub is associated with Raymond Moreno, partner of General Ver and uncle of Ching Escaler, is that Raymond is part of the treasure deal. Singlaub bought the maps, witness accounts, and an on-going treasure hunt operation from someone who insisted that Raymond's legal services be part of the deal. Ha. Ha. I bet that someone is General Ver. And I bet this crazy deal has been concocted to get some money out of the Moonies, a crazy cult that owns

the Washington Times and finances Causa International and the World Anti-Communist League."
February 26, 1987, Philippine Daily Inquirer

Part 6. Of Swards And Beautiful Dreamers

This is MAURICE ARCADIA the Arab Sheik, again writing as your society columnist. And the copy editor is warned not to change Sheik to Shriek, or Sikh or Sick ... otherwise he is going to get it in the donkey from the real Maurice.

Never mind what the dictionary says about the meaning of "sward". In the language of the young generation, "sward" means a male homosexual, a faggot, a badaf, a bakla, a syoki, in contrast to a dyke or lesbian, which is a female homosexual.

One night, our lavandero asked for the use of the Betamax and showed us a videotape of a Flores de Mayo where, to my surprise, I saw two of our household help, both males, parading around as females. JUDIWELO "Judy" RODRIGUEZ, our lavandero, and ARCHIE BELANDRES, our baker, declared that they are part of an organization of swards called "Beautiful Dreamers Association". No kidding.

Their president, MENCHU TOLENTINO, is an interior decorator, beautician, and the cook of PACITA DE LOS REYES PHILLIPS, former carnival queen, of Morado Street, Dasma. The vice president is EDNA REYES, mayordoma of the MANALO family of Narra, South Forbes.

The Treasurer is our own JUDY, and the assistant Treasurer is our own ARCHIE, so the money stays at our house.

The secretary is MONETTE TEVES, the cook of the MARQUINEZ family of Urdaneta Village. His/her Assistant is EDNA YCOT, a student of Fort Bonifacio High, where he/she is in the top ten of his/her class. He/she is the *kapatid*-in-law of DANNY SUAREZ, unsuccessful candidate for assemblyman in Laguna.

The PRO is GEMMA UGARTE, cook of Don JUAN CARLOS of Acacia, Dasma, and is known as the "bigotillo girl".

The sergeants-at-arms are JOSIE TOMATE, cook of GEORGE LITTON of Forbes, known as the "Bacolod Beauty";

and AN-AN ESPERANZA, cook of Dr. AUGUSTO "Toto" CAMARA, heart doctor who has garnered the highest grades ever given by the U.P. (1.008).

The Adviser is GLORIA KOREAN B., cook of PHILIP and CHING CRUZ of McKinley Road, who likes boys, but prefers girls, and has three children with the girls he encountered. He/she is known as "silahis".

The "Inductor" is a real doctor of medicine, Dr. EDDIE MAGNO, a graduate of the University of Los Angeles, and most respected among the sward community.

There are the ordinary members, of course. Central Bank Governor JOBO FERNANDEZ and wife TOTI contributed one cook in his household, MAXIMA CARPIO. Constitutional Commissioner CHRISTIAN MONSOD and wife WINNIE, contributed one cook, AMALIA DE LA RAMA.

Meralco's MANOLO LOPEZ of Harvard Street, Wack Wack, has also a cook, EMILY DE LEON; also ROMY and THELMA VILLONGCO of North Forbes, have cook ICTA PATONGERA; Dr. LEO LAZATIN of Carissa St., Dasma, has cook CRISTIE JENIFER; Mr. and Mrs. FELIPE FERNANDEZ of Calamansi, Dasma, have cook VANGIE CALVO; the MANALO family of Narra St., Forbes, has cook EDA PRADA; Mrs. MARIETTA SANTOS of Magnolia St., Dasma has BENILDA PEREGRINO, cook with a blonde wig, the "milagrosang Americana".

There are other than cooks: RHODORA NOLIKE, lavandera of GEORGE LITTON of Banaba St., Forbes, who is the "most promising 'badaf' of the year"; AURORA AFRIL, mayordoma of ex-Immigration Commissioner EDMUNDO and CARMEN REYES of Acacia Road, Dasma; PIA DEL PIERO, gardener of MERCEDES P. SISON of Tamarind St., Forbes.

And then the professionals: VICTORIA AMESTUOSO, medical attendant of the Philippine General Hospital; and TITA VISING, a house and lot owner of Alabang.

So I ask the guys/dolls: What is the purpose of their organization, aside from mutual protection and moral support? And they say, "Sssh, we spy on the CIA." I say, no kidding. And they say "Sssh, didn't you know that NORBERT GARRETT, the CIA boss, lives in Dasma with his SAMIA?" Samia, what's that? "Sssh, that's Garrett's second wife, she is an Arab, Lebanese we believe."

Yeah? What kind of a guy is this Norbert Garrett? Well, they say, "Sssh, wowie, goodness gracious, what a beautiful man -- 6 feet tall, light blonde, very goodlooking! Good enough to eat! Yum, yum, yum!"

Yeah, must have a beautiful house. "Sssh, it is full of television monitors, from the driveway to every bedroom, all recording into Betamax machines." Golly, an exhibitionist, eh? One of those secretly yearning to be in the movies, eh? "Sssh, he's got an arsenal too of all sorts of handguns, machine guns, grenade launchers. Sssh, I think he is a colleague of ex-Ambassador BIENVENIDO TANTOCO."

But what is the purpose of Garrett? I thought the Philippines is already safe American-occupied territory. "Sssh, all that hardware is to protect SAMIA GARRETT and their 6-year old boy from being contaminated by Filipinos." No kid. "Sssh, Samia the Arab, barely 5 feet, with dyed blonde hair, looking like the sister of Omar Shariff, insists that wherever she goes, the place must be sanitized and sterilized. Sssh, she won't allow her son to talk to drivers or security guards, unless they first take a bath in alcohol. She thinks every Filipino carries bacteria and bombs like the Lebanese."

Listen, Samia could not be that bad, she is an Arab Lebanese like me, Maurice Arcadia, and everybody knows that Beirut is a much cleaner and much safer place than Manila. Can you blame her for being apprehensive about the safety and well-being of her little son?

Anyway CHRISTINE BOSWORTH, also second wife of the Ambassador, is much better. "Sssh, yes, yes, yes, Christine is a good housewife, cooks very well, and prepares meals for that stuff-shirt STEVE BOSWORTH." No kid, do you think we can get her to slip the guy a Mickey Finn?" Sssh, no way. "Sssh, Christine is going to write a book on native foods, featuring her favorite dish, Sliced LARRY HENARES on rye. Sssh, she's okay, she likes Filipinos --- goes around with AMELITA GUEVARA and CARMINA DE LEON, both pianists, and even goes dancing with Trebel prexy BERT DEL ROSARIO and accompanist JOSEFINA VELOSO." No kidding. "Sssh, yeah!"

Hey, you guys/dolls are mostly cooks, are you not? What's your favorite dish? "We swards love our donkeys and we feed them a lot of hot salami." How do you serve the salami, sliced? "Of course not, what do you think our donkeys are --- piggie banks?" And he/she laughs and laughs and laughs, and I still do not get it.

How did you get to be a sward? "My fault, I used to be a real man till I fiddled around my boss' bathroom which he filled with many modern gadgets. I sat down on his toilet seat, and saw this little red button beside it with a sign DO NOT TOUCH. I said to myself, my boss is not around to get mad anyway, so why not press the little red button to satisfy my curiousity? I did, and the next thing I knew I was in the hospital, a complete sward! All because I pressed the wrong button."

Why, what was it for? "It was an automatic Tampax Extractor and Disposal Unit!"

Do you know any bosses in Dasma who are also swards? "Well, one of the sons of my boss is a real sward. Early in the morning, he brings to office two handkerchiefs, one embroidered and one ordinary one: one for show, and one for blow. When he gets to the office, he has two secretaries to serve him, one good looking young girl, and one very good looking young man: one for show, one for blow."

The Beautiful Dreamers Association holds parties every Saturday, rain or shine, usually in Harvard Street, Wack Wack Village, Mandaluyong, most probably in the compound of MANOLO LOPEZ. One special occasion was the birthday of AURORA AFRIL who gave a party in Acacia Road, Dasmarinas; only a few people attended because non-Dasma guests were not allowed in. No permit was issued because the owner of the house, MUNDING REYES, is a Marcos loyalist. That's really dung!

Then there was the wedding party in Barrio Trece, Tanza, Cavite, where MENCHU TOLENTINO, AMALIA DE LA RAMA, ICTA PANTOGERA, JUDY RODRIGUEZ, ARCHIE BELANDRES, BENILDA PEREGRINA, and RHODORA NOLIKE were invited. They danced and danced till 3 a.m., when they all retired with friends to a cottage, and in Judy's words, "floated in the sky of happiness."

Homosexuals abound in families where (1) there is an overpossessive dominant mother, and a weak father-figure, or (2) there is a playboy macho father who browbeats the mother and openly keeps *queridas*. Check it out among your friends, you will find that playboy machos have homosexuals among their children.   Several examples come to mind, but they better be left unsaid, or we'll get a beating on our donkeys.

Swards come in different forms: (1) transvestites, who like to wear women's dresses, but are not necessarily true homosexuals; (2) trans-sexuals, men who undergo a sex change operation like Christian/Christine Jorgenson; (3) queens, who exhibit the most feminine characteristics such as limp wrists, swaying hips and a loud gossipy nagging voice; (4) machoqueens,who are usually athletes attracted to group contact sports such as football and basketball where they are in contact with other men; (5) closet queens, who are usually married, with children, and do their stuff on the sly.

In the United States and elsewhere, most gay relationships are between two swards, one taking the role of the boy and the other the girl.   Which is which depends on who has the stronger personality.   Swards therefore may reverse roles from partner to partner, depending on the relative dominance of one partner over the other.

Filipino swards, however, like the Beautiful Dreamers, prefer real men whom they recruit among the *bagets* from 16 to 20 years old, and ply with cigarettes, clothes, money, even drugs.   In the Villages, the usual targets for companionship are the ever-present guards with whom the swards have a love-hate relationship.   The guards (who also are popular among the maids) have to contend with prowling swards in the dead of night, despite village curfew regulations.   The guards like to have the swards around during the lonely hours.   At the same time the guards exploit the poor swards by beating them up, extorting from them money and possessions and what pathetically passes off for love and affection.

But relations between swards and straights are seldom permanent; so; in the higher income levels, in the world of artists, actors, couturiers, and other professionals, the gay-to-gay relationship is preferred.

Among the most creative and sensitive and lovable persons are those in the movie and theater world --- like actors BERNARDO BERNARDO, and FREDDIE SANTOS who admit to being bisexual; and movie directors BEHN CERVANTES, ISHMAEL BERNAL, MANING BORLAZA --- whose understanding of the nuances of both sexes contribute much to moving portrayals on screen and stage, of the tragic vulnerability of the human condition.

FANNY SERRANO, Dr. REY DE LA CRUZ ("mother" of soft drink bomba stars), BABETTE CORQUERA, SOXY TOPACIO are swards who make it by honestly playing themselves.

Portraying sward roles in movies and television to tickle our funny bone are such superb straight artists as DOLPHY, MICHAEL DE MESA, RODERICK PAULATE, DINDO FERNANDO, VIC SOTTO, JOEY DE LEON, EDDIE GARCIA, EDDIE RODRIGUEZ, PANCHITO ALBA.

Swards exist, you know, in the devil's world of religious bigots, along with abortionists and divorcees. How will BERNIE VILLEGAS and the Moral Judges of the ConCom deal with them in the new Constitution? Take it easy, Bernie; you probably do your own cooking, but sward cooks have control over the food we eat, including that of CHRISTIAN and JOBO.

October 12, 1986, Sunday Inquirer

Part 7. Manglapus' rascals; Red Skelton; slay the father-image

FOREIGN secretary Raul Manglapus announced that he favors treaty negotiating panels.

Excellent idea, if we have a clear concept of what negotiation is all about.

First, we must not have a negotiator who is "acceptable" to the other side, or we may find ourselves saddled with "double allegiance."

Guys like Small Dick, Little Brown Jug-Ears, Uncle Tom, Alopecic Gynander, Narding Siguion Reyna, Sali Salazar have represented foreigners too long, and should be spared the embarrassment of negotiating with present and future clients.

Second, a negotiator need not be an expert. He needs to have resource persons who are. Ongpin, Jobo and Virata are good resource persons, but they are lousy negotiators, because they have the tendency to favor the American side..

Third, a negotiator must have a combative personality, just like Max Kempelman now negotiating nuclear disarmament with the Soviets in Geneva. Max learns all about the fellow on the other side, exploring and exploiting his weaknesses -- women, liquor, chess, coin collection -- in off-hours.

A negotiator must know when to practice brinkmanship or walk-out; he must know how to bluff, deceive, threaten, pretend injury, fake boredom, raise his voice, ask for more than he expects to get, enjoy the give-and-take of bargaining, and throw the kitchen sink.

When Kokoy Romualdez negotiated the bases treaty with Michael Armacost, the Americans were nudging and winking at each other at the prospect of easy victory. As usual, Armacost spoke about security against external aggression. As usual Kokoy looked as if he could not understand College English.

Then Kokoy interrupted: "Let us talk of something else. How about the social cost of the bases -- the AIDS, herpes, gonorrhea, syphilis; drugs, nightclubs, prostitution; abandoned sweethearts, wives, babies; honky-tonks, GI crimes; American flag on our soil, tax-free PX goods that compete with our industries; privileges and extraterritorial rights; base rentals grudgingly and niggardly doled out on `best efforts' basis."

Marcos wanted $500 million, Kokoy got $900 million, the first time he did us any good.

We do not need a goody-goody like Pelaez to negotiate for us.

What we need is a rascal ... to deal effectively with the rascals on the other side.

* * *

Nina Puyat once said that I can paint pictures with words.

I write of Gino Padilla ending his song with his fist hanging on to a piece of the sky, and of a bed as a gateway to the land of dreams.

Nina says I project my thoughts like a movie, putting faces on generalities, caricatures like Garrett for the CIA, Ongpin for the IMF, Buenaventura for foreign interests.

Today I shall project the image of Tourism Secretary Jose Antonio Gonzalez.

Tony is the son-in-law of old friend MIT-educated Tito Sevilla; employer of my cousin Dulce, wife of Sen. Rene Saguisag; nemesis of cousin Sylvia Lichauco; and boss of Jun

Campillo, whose name Sostenes is Spanish for brassiere.

As Speedy Gonzalez, Tony is all over the place, like the cartoon character as he speeds away, "Andale! Andale! Andale!" living it up in every jet-set watering hole in the world, convinced that being a Tourism Secretary means being the Number One tourist of the Philippines.

I like him because of his indefatigable good humor in the face of daily assaults by his Immensity; his permanent smile amidst coups and assassinations.

Why is it that every time we see Tony, we cannot help laughing? On television one day we scrutinized him.

We look at his eyes. Sometimes they wink in mischief like a naughty child's ... sometimes they turn quizzical as if they cannot puzzle out the Immensity's obsession ... sometimes the two eyes refuse to cooperate with each other and turn a bit cross-eyed.

We look at his lips. The lower lips sometimes pout ... sometimes flip and flap ... and then collapse into a wide and silly grin, bracketed by dimples.

Imagine Tony Gonzalez, befuddled and nursing a tall glass of whisky ... on his head a felt hat with its front brim flipped up ... with crossed eyes and a silly grin ... staggering on rubber legs over to the bar --

By golly, he is the spitting image of our favorite comedian Red Skelton!

That is why we like Speedy Gonzalez, he is so funny. We shall enjoy having lunch with him.

* * *

Emerita Sevilla, when you meet me, embrace me, Ces wouldn't mind. I love your letter to the editor (PDI, Oct.19). You really got my number but not quite.

You see, Emerit, I am not a referee or judge or arbiter. I am a protaganist, a combatant, I am a player on the Filipino team. In combat, I am not supposed to be nice.

I am the bad guy like Starsky, so you and others can play the good guy Hutch.

When a foreigner is mean and unfair and gives the Filipino the boot, I see to it he knows what it feels to be kicked too, even as you lecture him nicely about good manners.

I spoke of my fight before the Monetary Board against ten American companies importing paint. Oldtimer Jack

Manning was saying that "Henares paint is lousy, nobody wants it."

No matter how nice and logical I was, showing comparative test results of my paint and theirs, the Board actually believed Jack (being an American), though he had no proof.

I remembered my school debates, and realized Jack was employing *argumentum ad autoritatem*, "I say so, therefore it must be so!" to which the only effective answer is *argumentum ad hominem*, "And who the hell do you think you are?"

I corrected his memo for grammatical errors; challenged him to an IQ and math test; and belittled his education. And won my case.

Americans may be nice as Spanish priests were nice, but we must as Rizal did, as Manglapus urged, "slay the father image," -- and strip them of their immunities and privileges ... of their mantle of authority and pretensions to superiority.

After my article on Jo Brady Garabato, I doubt if any American reader will ever again shout at a Filipina.
October 21, 1987, Philippine Daily Inquirer

Part 8. Arab terrorism invades San Lorenzo

ON Holy Thursday, at 5:45 AM, in San Lorenzo Village Park, a greasy two-bit Arab, half naked with a dog-chain around his neck to show what a dog he is, with three unidentified companions, under the very eyes of security guards, tore down, defaced and destroyed the campaign posters of barangay candidates for Kagawad: Dr. Romulo Trinidad, my uncle Atty. Tony Nieva, Cely Topacio, Joey Coronel, Abelardo Yabut and Julio Locsin.

Looking like Incredible Hulk and Mr. T combined, this blubber of a man, went back to his cave in Arguilla street where he stays with his father a overstaying Lebanese with a Hitler mustache. All this, according to Architect Toti Mendoza who was last seen at the US Embassy for political asylum from what he termed Arab terrorism in San Lorenzo. He identified the terrorist as Mark Joseph. the son of Mike Joseph.

All I am saying is that if anything happens to my friend

Toti, this Arab terrorist and his blubber of a son are going to find their asses smeared all over the front pages, and the whole Armed Forces shoving bayonets up their intestines.

This is too much. It is bad enough that my friend, Rep. Moises Espinosa, was wasted, iced, terminated with extreme prejudice in the wilds of Masbate airport. But to have the same lunacy in the heart of Makati is intolerable. I suggest that our favorite Mayor Jojo Binay, send his zoo-keepers to inject these Arabs with anti-rabies serum and get them back into cages where they belong.

I cannot understand how Jojo, whom I admire as a man of perception and defender of human rights, would have in his barangay ticket an Arab goon, a gun smuggler and a crapulous lush pickled in alcohol -- three ideal candidates for barangay elections in Bilibid Prison, but not in San Lorenzo Village.

Come on, Tini Pertierra, Justice Jose Feria, retired Ambassadors Constante Cruz, Tom de Castro and Alberto Katigbak, my favorite Foreign Secretary Raul Manglapus, Gloria Diaz Dazed, poet Rafael Zulueta de Costa, Salvador Estrada, Congressman Enrique Garcia of Bataan, Staffmen of Opus Dei at Melantic Street, Doña Elena Roensch Lichauco Small, Assumption nuns, neuro-surgeon Dr. Victor Reyes, bean-pole Victor Lim, lawyer Oscar Domingo, Atty. Jose Lao -- all ye denizens of San Lorenzo. Arise and vote out these goons.

On the other hand, the barangay elections in the other villages, particularly in Forbes and Dasma, there is such a dearth of candidates that the positions to be filled are equal to the candidates running. And these candidates had to be cajoled, and pushed into running.

There must be something in San Lorenzo Village that makes being a councilor or a Kagawad or a village association official such a prize to be fought for by goons, smugglers and inebriates.

San Lorenzo is second oldest Ayala village (Forbes is first). Its barangay comprises not only the village itself but also Legaspi Village, the Makati Commercial Center, Greenbelt and half of Ayala Avenue, the Wall Street of the Philippines. It is the richest barangay in the entire Philippines, with a total annual revenue collection of billions of pesos, of which P1.1 million is under the control of the barangay Kagawad of seven councilmen -- enough to buy guns and hire goons as the proper perquisites of political power.

Other Makati villages have their covered basketball courts, their streets paved, dredging of their esteros, at the expense of the barangay -- but not in San Lorenzo, the richest of all barangays. You go to San Lorenzo and it looks seedy and worn down, although real estate values have gone up to P7,000 per square meter (Forbes and Dasma properties are P10,000 per square meter). Where does the money go?

Can you beat it? San Lorenzo is the first reported election hot spot in Makati -- right in the heart of our financial district and prime residential area.

We hope the television crews and radiomen and press reporters will saturate the area today, and keep a eye on the Arab terrorist, the gun smuggler and the crapulous souse, and see that they behave like civilized human beings instead of the armpits of society that they are.

The San Lorenzo Village Association opened up their gates on Amorsolo Street from Pasay Road to Edsa, to ease traffic flow for those who travel from Makati to the South Expressway, and it does not get any help from the barangay for the repair of this vital artery.

The transients working in Makati during the day, who contribute to the tremendous income of this premier town, deserve more from the voters of Makati. The transients who work in the large offices in barangay San Lorenzo deserve a better service than anything an Arab terrorist, a smuggler and a souse can offer.

Come on, San Lorenzo, wake up. And vote right.
March 27, 198, Philippine Daily Inquirer 9

ooooo

PERSPECTIVES

ooooo

CHAPTER 1. How To Serve Americans

INTRO: a letter from a reader, ENRIQUE VELASCO, Guerrero Street, Makati

March 28, 1988, The Editor, Philippine Daily Inquirer, Manila

Dear sir: Correct me if I am wrong but the persons being always referred to in Henares' column, Make My Day, are:

- Arroyo, Joker: The Big Joke
- Bengzon, Alran: St. Alran, The Saint
- Bengzon, Jose: Little Brown Jug-ears
- Bernas, Joaquin: Doc, Rasputin
- Buenaventura, Cesar: Our Man Squint, Convexity of his Face
- Fernandez, Jobo: Pompous Ass
- Jayme, Vicente: The Big Sleep
- Locsin, Teddyboy: Teodorus Filius, Theopolous, The Finger
- Macaraig, Catalino: Mac the Knife, Father of Twink
- Mangahas, Majar: Mumbles
- Monsod, Christian: Uncle Tom, Tom Hearns, Raging Bull
- Monsod, Solita: Screaming Banshee, Wicked Witch of the West, Holy Cow
- Nieva, Teresa: Sta. Teresa, Our Lady of Zeroes
- Platt, Nicholas: Hoy Kulas, Jeeves the Butler
- Reyes, Rainerio: Pile of Pomade
- Romulo, Ricardo: Small Dick
- Soriano, Noel: Walter Mitty, Goldfinger, Dopey
- Villegas, Bernardo: Alopecic Gynander

March 28, 1988, Philippine Daily Inquirer

Part 1. How To Serve Americans

I am writing a book entitled HOW TO SERVE AMERICANS, which I am sure will be a best-seller.

Remember the old Catholic catechism before Vatican II Council? Question: What is the purpose of our existence? Answer: Our purpose is to love God, to serve Him in this world, and to be happy with Him forever in the next.

Well, there is another version which should be inserted in the new Constitution. Question: What is the purpose of the existence of Filipino citizens? Answer: Our purpose is to love Americans, to serve them in the Philippines, and to be happy with them Stateside as a green card holders or TNT.

Let's face it. According to reliable surveys, 90% of our children and 60% of our adults would rather be American citizens than Filipino citizens, and sacrifice themselves to keep Americans happy, hi-falutin, prosperous and free.

We honor most those Filipinos who serve Americans and foreigners best. We honor Jimmy Ongpin because he is a trusted colleague of Herbert Allen; Monetary Board member Cesar Buenaventura who is being pushed by Jimmy to take the place of Executive Secretary Joker Arroyo, because he works for Shell Company; CocoBank president and probable successor to Jimmy Ongpin or Jobo Fernandez --- the favored Ramon Siy -- because he used to be vice president of the Bank of America; in the ConCom. Bernie Villegas because he is in the Time magazine Board of Economists, Ricardo Romulo because he is servicing a clientele of some 40 foreign corporations, Christian Monsod because he used to work for the World Bank. They all belong to the same Sodality that worships Americans, and calls the shots in the world of business.

In this country, our choices for key positions in the cabinet must have American approval, or at least no American objection: the Foreign Minister, the Finance Minister, Defense Minister, Chief of Staff, Ambassador to Washington.

Sometime in 1983-84, when the Monetary Board was negotiating a moratorium of interest payments to foreign creditors, the CityBank was accepting dollar deposits and borrowing a lot of dollars from clients who assumed that CityBank's dollar obligations may be paid from any Citybank branch in the world. When the moratorium came into effect, CityBank announced that it is a Filipino corporation, and is therefore not obligated to pay interest under the moratorium.

There were court suits, amid allegations that the CityBank president Rafael Buenaventura, the brother of Cesar the Monetary Board Member, had advance information on the moratorium, and acted unethically to gain unfair advantage.

But no investigation was made, on the ground that Rafael did not personally gain from this breach of ethics, and did so only unselfishly for the benefit of CityBank. If he were not working for an American bank, Rafael would have been raked over the coals, but apparently rendering service to Americans is the highest duty of a Filipino.

Those who serve American or IMF interests are handsomely rewarded. The Marcos technocrats who delivered the economy to the multinationals and the IMF are not doing badly. NEDA chief Gerry Sicat is now a minor official of the World Bank; his successor Vicente Valdepenas is a highly paid consultant to the Bank of America; Prime Minister Cesar Virata is a highly paid consultant of the World Bank. Jimmy Ongpin who is an unabashed defender of Americans and the IMF, was appointed Finance Minister and became an instant multimillionaire when his Benguet shares was bought from him at P42.00 at the time the market value was only P24.00 per share.

In 1964-65, I had a cousin who worked for Wyeth Laboratories. His American boss received a shipment of heart medicine, Digitalis, way beyond its date of expiration; the boss ordered it sold to Chinese clients. My cousin who is an American citizen reported it and a raid was conducted to seize the spoiled merchandise. A few days later the seized goods were released upon intervention of a high official and upon representation of the company's lawyers, Sycip/Salazar; and my cousin Eric Sollee was sent back to the States in disgrace.

I had an American classmate in M.I.T. who constantly borrowed my notes and wore out my shirts, and did not get to finish the course till long after I graduated. For sometime he lived in a one-room cold-water flat in the seedy side of New York. Then all of a sudden he wangled a job in a multinational company in the Philippines. Lucky guy, all of a sudden he lived in Forbes Park and was welcomed into the elegant society of cosmopolitan Manila.

He would not even deign to say hello to me. Neither did he offer to replace my shirts.

The book I am writing, HOW TO SERVE AMERICANS, will be in the bookstores soon. It is a cook book, and the best part of it deals with serving *Adobong Americano,* made by

marinating American ambassadors in soy sauce, garlic, vinegar and salt.
September 9, 1986, Philippine Daily Inquirer

Part 2. CIS Agent Manny Ortaleza guilty of treason?

PATRIOTISM and nationalism are words that are not interchangeable. Patriotism is an emotion, nationalism is an intellectual concept. Patriotism means love of country and its people. Nationalism is faith in one's own countrymen, faith in their capacity for greatness, and in their competence to take care of their own affairs.

It is possible to be a patriot without being a nationalist. But one has to be a patriot to be a true nationalist. No one doubts that President Manuel Roxas was a patriot, who gave Americans military bases and parity rights because he believed they were good for the Filipino people; but he was not a nationalist. Claro M. Recto by decrying parity rights and the Bases, proved himself to be both a patriot and a nationalist.

Those in the ConCom, like Christian Monsod, Dick Romulo, Bernie Villegas and Ted Bacani who voted for American Bases and a colonial type of plantation economy, may claim to be patriots, but they certainly are not nationalists, because they did not have faith in the Filipino's capacity to stand alone without the help of the American imperialists.

Nationalism presupposes that we Filipinos belong to each other and to something greater than ourselves, the nation; and that we must unite to promote, protect and defend our interests in the same way that Americans promote, protect and defend their interests. To promote the interest of another nation at the expense of our own, is treachery and treason.

On Friday, September 16, 1988, Manny Ortaleza and others, Criminal Investigation Service (CIS) agents of the Philippine Constabulary, under orders from Colonel Piad and Major Zacarias reportedly committed treachery. They betrayed Christopher Barredo, a fellow Filipino, took custody of him without warrant of arrest, and turned him over to agents of the US Military. The Americans brought Chris to the Subic Naval Base, and airlifted him to Okinawa to face a court martial for being absent without official leave (AWOL) from the

US Marines.

Christopher Barredo was taken by Manny Ortaleza and other CIS agents, armed with pistols and armalites, at the Land Bank where he was with the stage crew and cast of Repertory Philippines' "La Cage Aux Folles." In the presence of Joy Virata (Cesar's wife), Bernardo Bernardo, and Jaime Blanche, he was taken without an arrest order.

Christopher Barredo, son of Charlie and nephew of Baby Barredo our Queen of the Theater, protested that he was a Filipino citizen, with a US green card, who came back to the Philippines on a Philippine passport.

Again and again, he told them he is a Filipino citizen, and offered to show them his passport at home. But he was not even accorded the chance to present the proof.

He was held at Camp Crame for several hours till the American agents of the US Naval Intelligence Service (NIS) arrived. He then was arrested by these foreign agents for being AWOL and shipped off to Okinawa for court martial.

Even granting that Christopher was guilty in the eyes of the US Marines, the CIS agent Manny Ortaleza has no right to take him into custody without a warrant of arrest, or allow him to be shipped abroad without extradition proceedings, without being informed of his rights, without due process and benefit of counsel.

Christopher is a Filipino and he has constitutional rights in his own country. Anyone who betrays him to a foreign power is a traitor.

The trouble with some people in the military is that their primary allegiance is to a country not their own, snapping to attention and saluting every white-assed neanderthal that passes by, and taking orders from Americans as if it were the most natural thing in the world.

Well, it is about time that they are made to realize that their allegiance is to the Filipino people who pay their salaries; that they are not Little Brown Americans serving as pro-consuls or surrogates or cannon fodder for the American military; that betraying their countrymen is Treason, a crime much worse than carnapping, bank-robbing, bullying bar girls, rape and murder, that CIS agents are often accused of.

Secretary Eddie Ramos and Chief of Staff de Villa are always talking about getting rid of the scalawags and stinkers in the army, police and the constabulary. Well, here's Colonel Piad, Major Zacarias, and CIS agent Manny Ortaleza who should be court-martialed for for treason and violation of human rights.

And if found guilty, they should be tarred and feathered, drawn and quartered, and drummed out of the service, if not actually hanged for acts worthy of Benedict Arnold and Judas Iscariot.

But they probably won't be, because most of their superiors feel the same way about Americans. Dung.
April 28, 1989, Philippine Daily Inquirer

Part 3. MNC lackeys owe debt to nationalists

WHEN a nation fights against foreign domination, many of her own citizens side with the enemy. During the American Revolution, these were the Tories, among whom was Benedict Arnold.

In Mexico, they were the Malinches, named after Aztec princess Malinche, the whore of Conquistador Hernando Cortes, who with him plotted the extermination of her own people.

In the Philippine Revolution they were the Macabebes.

Today we have them in the Makati Business Club (MBC), a coven of pro-American lackeys mostly in the payroll of foreign companies, and proudly so.

For they feel that having attained their position in competition with the whites, they have proven themselves superior to the rest of us Filipinos.

Filipinos anointed to head the multinationals (MNCS) are Cesar Buenaventura of Shell; Amaury Gutierrez and Frankie Ablan of Caltex; Rafael Buenaventura and Joe Facundo of Citibank; Jimmy Ongpin and Del Lazaro of Benguet; Rainerio Reyes and Bobby Romulo of IBM.

Our Man Squint, cousin Cesar Buenaventura, could have had any government position for the asking, had he not wanted to wait for his retirement pay, they say, of more than $1 million.

In the acquisitive world of the MBC, where a man's worth is measured by the money he makes, Cesar is considered greater than Ninoy Aquino and Jose Rizal combined, though lesser than Jaime Zobel.

I got news for Cesar and his friends. None of them could have risen above the status of clerks, had not the nationalists fought to do away with discrimination in foreign companies.

For Filipino employees of foreign companies, the turning point came in April 1965, when Filipino executives declared a strike demanding equal pay for equal work, at Caltex, a block away from my National Economic Council (NEC) office.

Alejandro Lichauco, NEC policy director, was often at the picket line. I supported the strike in my front page column in the Manila Times, and in hearings at the "`Equal Pay for Equal Work."

- At the time, in Caltex, 22 executives received more (P2,257,034.10) in annual salaries than 136 Filipino executives did (P2,013,320.00). The average salary of a foreign executive was more than six times that of a Filipino.

- The highest paid Filipino, vice-president J.P. Roxas, also board member, second only to the top, was paid LOWER than the lowest paid of 22 foreigners. He was paid P44,000, while the lowest paid American (called the Squaw Man because he married a Filipina) was Raymond Wilmark, paid P44,515. The second lowest paid foreigner was a Spaniard, Raul Melian, who was a technical assistant to a department manager, paid P62,570.07. The third lowest was a fag called Robert Hinchman, advertising manager, paid P76,979.96.

- The highest paid foreigner was president William E. Menefee, J.P. Roxas' immediate boss, with a salary of P163,876.19, almost four times as large than Roxas' (P44,000). Vice-president J.G. Schaberg, American, was paid P139,940, three times as large as vice-president Roxas'.

- Three Filipino department managers received P32,400 (public relations, Dr. Jose L. Mathay); P22,128 (sales promotion, Cres Asuncion); P22,644 (government accounts, D.B. Ramirez). Their foreign counterparts received P112,385 (national accounts, G. Barberan, Spaniard); and P76,979.96 (advertising, R. Hinchman).

- Three Filipino district managers received P24,960 (E.V. Bernardino), P21,360 (F.S. Tecson), P21,300 (J. Rafols). One foreign district manager received P91,296 (M.O.

Pritchett, Australian); a mere asst. district manager received P91,296 (R.A. Kimball, American).

- A Filipino Technical assistant to the department manager received P22,044 (M.T. Feliciano). His foreign counterpart received P62,570.07 (Raul Melian, Spaniard).

NEC condemned Caltex for racial discrimination. Labor unions and students joined the picket line. The Diokno-Tañada Bill passed both Houses, but the Embassy and an American lobby group called Philippine Association headed by Small Dick Romulo's father, got the President to veto it, on their promise that there will be no more discrimination.

In 45 days the strike ended. And all Filipinos in Caltex and elsewhere got a fair shake.

Cesar and the rest of you lackeys in the Makati Business Club, you owe us nationalists a big debt, and don't you ever forget it!

August 3, 1988, Philippine Daily Inquirer

Part 4. Doy Laurel's secret list of rightist fascists

ACCORDING to unreliable sources, Doy Laurel the McCarthyist is not taking any chances.

If he cannot be president of the Fifth Republic, then he aspires to be in the ruling junta of Honasan.

Failing that, he may turn far left and be the Political Commissar of the Philippines.

Failing that, he may even turn Jap collaborator, shogun of Japan's Greater East Asia Co-Prosperity Sphere.

As a last recourse he may swear allegiance to the Philippine flag and constitution, and turn nationalist as his revered father was ... if nationalists will elevate him to the presidency.

In the remotest chance that the nationalists, under the inspiration of Rizal, Recto and Ninoy Aquino, take over and throw out the American bases, Doy is reportedly prepared to expose a secret list of rightist fascists given to him by no less than Norbert Garrett, CIA station chief.

Noring Garrett insists that the list is unofficial, contains raw data and is a working draft that need no permission from Ambassador Kulas to pass on to Doy Laurel the official US-designated McCarthyist.

On top of the fascist list is brother Senator Sotero Laurel who resents not being included in the Doy's list of leftists and commies ... who unlike Doy, studied in UP instead of La Salle, Harvard instead of Yale ... who, Doy suspects, remains faithful to wife Lorna, and refrains from sowing wilds oats in greener pastures.

Next is another brother Ambassador Jose Laurel III who also happens to be a faithful husband.

Not that Doy has anything against faithful husbands.

Next on the list of fascist rightists are those with a seven-year itch ... Tony Speedy Gonzalez, Ernie Maceda, Johnny Ponce Enrile, Arturo Tolentino ... as well as such wives as Mrs. Tolentino, Mrs. Tolentino, and Mrs. Tolentino.

Nor is Doy prejudiced against the Celibates ... CRC's Bernie Villegas of the decorticated pate, and DBP's Jesus Estanislao with his properly pomaded fuzz, who actually live in boys' dormitories away from the opposite sex ... BOI's Tom Alcantara who at his age is running out of excuses for not getting married ... Bishop Ted Bacani whose views in the ConCom prompted an activist nun to exclaim, "The trouble with you, bishop, is that you have never been raped!" ... and of course, Ricardo Cardinal Vidal, and our favorite humorist Jaime Cardinal Sin with his gentle remonstrances against nationalist lepers, liberated women, and Ginny Lichauco de Leon.

Also on the list is the Council of Trent, which is headed by the Shell's Villainous Convexity of a Face, and Benguet's Concavity of a Face, CB's Pompous Ass, MBC chairman Small Dick, BBC chairman Uncle Tom Hearns who wants to be PNB president, MAP president Joe Facundo of the City Trust ... the latest oligarchs of this country.

Oligarchs come from a long line of balimbings in this country ... salivators of the *gluteus maximus* of every government official from Danding Romualdez to Fenny Hechanova to Gregorio Licaros to Bobby Ongpin ... contributing to all political parties and candidates regardless of persuasion, even to Marcos ... and held together by their loyalty to Mother America and the Almighty Dollar.

Today, led by the Concavity and Convexity, they throw their weight around, hiding behind the skirts of the bishops, and pushing the president around because she happens to be a girl and because in their world, girls are only good enough for serving coffee.

Someday, Cory will have to put them back in their places.

Among the press, Doy the McCarthyist has a long list of rightist fascists.

I head the list because I am a bit overweight and do not have the lean and hungry look of a real revolutionary ... besides I am the favorite of Queen Bea Zobel ... therefore I must be a Spanish Royalist and a bloated capitalist. I protest.

With me on the list is Maximus Sullivan who has walked with more heroes than Romulo himself, and with more heels than Adidas ... the Kennedy brothers, Ngo Dinh Diem, Bung Karno, Indira Gandhi, Golde Meir, Nassr, Aguinaldo, Marcos, Shah of Iran, Eisenhower, Johnson, Nixon, Eldon Cruz ... Max knew them all, by golly!

And of course wherever Max is, the Immensity is sure to follow ... his friends are Ernie Maceda, Fabian Ver, and also Joker Arroyo ... but those are enough to land him in Doy's fascist list.

Well, there are others in the list, according to unreliable sources ... my friend Ramon Tulfo who thinks every revolution is a purgative to get rid of the unfit in our society ... Nestor Mata who was the only one to survive the Magsaysay air crash ... Melchor Aquino, Beth Day, press relations officers like Dennis Navarro and Adi Sison ... and many others.

Then there are the RAMboys and their sympathizers ... Col. Gringo Honasan, Col. Red Capunan, Captain Rex Robles, Col. Cabauatan ... those in the PMA who follow the West Point traditions of Duty, Honor, Country, the latter being the United States rather than the Philippines ... and those in the Armed Forces who prattle about leftists, nationalists opposing American bases and IMF as being subversives, and who consider clerico fascists, rightists and Filipino CIA agents as believers in democracy.

There are the Marcos loyalists who are pro-American and therefore, pro-democracy.

Then the GAD oppositionists headed by Kit Tatad and Rene Espina.

Finally there are the presidential relatives -- Tessie Aquino Oreta, Ding Tanjuatco, Peping Cojuangco, Komong

Sumulong.

Doy Laurel does not miss a trick. The leftist and rightist lists are not the only ones he has; he is preparing a third list.

For his American friends, in case they would like to repeat their feat in Samar some 90 years ago, Doy Laurel is making a computerized list of ALL Filipinos, man, woman, and child down to ten years old, that will make the task easier for Americans to make the Philippines a "howling wilderness," as General Smith did.

October 7, 1987, Philippine Daily Inquirer

Part 5.   When the first American rascal met the first Filipino fool

LONG AGO, I received an anonymous letter directed against ex-Senator Emmanuele Pelaez so libelous I threw it into the waste-basket. Months later, Pelaez was machine-gunned in his car. He woke up in the hospital with the understatement of the year, "have no known enemies."

Every day I receive anonymous letters about such people as Ramon Diaz, Clipper Lorenzo, Raul Roco, Marycon Bautista, Solita Monsod, columnist Max Sullivan; the love life of Jobo Fernandez, of Christian Monsod (imagine!), of Joker Arroyo, of the Immensity; even one article about myself, sent in by a friend, but without any claim of authorship on the article itself. Such are the stuff of which libel suits are made.

Several letters come from alleged members of the Silliman University Alumni Association, detailing the sins of PCGG Commissioner Quintin Doromal. The signatures are illegible, obviously from the same hand and deliberately disguised.

Poison pen letters are trash. They are products of sick and fevered minds, of cowards and poltroons.

We columnists have an obligation to criticize the high and the mighty, to expose or prevent shenanigans and chicanery among those who abuse with impunity. The constitution guarantees freedom of the press and of information.

But we are not immune from libel suits. His Immensity boasts of 42 libel suits; Ramon Tulfo I understand has eleven cases; I have only one, which my lawyer says is nothing. My lawyer also says that no libel suit against the press has ever been successful in this country.

Every so often we columnists must take stock of how we use our press freedom, that we might not be ourselves guilty of abuse.

I am not altogether innocent, I am sure. I believe my attacks against the pro-American acts and actuations of public figures are legitimate criticisms. My descriptions of Jimmy's concavity of a face, Bernie's decorticated pate and Jobo's pompous ass, are not.

But they were meant to be facetious, written with tongue in cheek, not in malice but in mischief. I mean, that part about Christian being knocked out by Winnie, is so patently apocryphal that no one should believe it. But some people do. And to that extent I must apologize to Christian and Winnie.

Winnie says, "The only reason I tolerate Larry is because of his wonderful children." I feel the same way about Christian's kids. One time Tammy sent me a mass card for the salvation of my soul, and I was so touched that I wrote her a note thanking her and Toby, and asking that they arrange a breakfast meeting with their father, so we can thresh out our differences and be friends once more. Nothing came of it. But the offer is still good.

I have to remind myself of what my Jesuit mentors taught me -- that great movements require passion and compassion. Passion for ideas and compassion for our fellowmen.

We do need great passion, all our resources of caring, loving, hating, to fire both reason and conscience to judge, to acclaim, and to denounce. But such passion becomes twisted and ugly when it seeks not cause but blame, not reason but victims, not discernment and understanding but punishment.

That is why the rage or revenge of American super-patriots, of angry champions of any extreme, whether urban guerillas or fascistic army agents and vigilantes, armored in hate, always threatens the ways of freedom.

Tyranny always defends itself by directing its passions against men. And by its own pitiless logic, it exiles, it tortures, it burns, it shoots, it hurls a bomb. Marcos and the Shah with their torture chambers, Khaddafi and Khomeini and the Klu Klux Klan with their hired assassins, Reagan and Gorbachev with their CIA and KGB -- they are all birds of the same feather.

We Filipinos must do otherwise.

We must keep passion within the realm of ideas. And compassion in our relations with our fellowmen. We must love the dictator even as we hate dictatorship. We must love the murderer even as we hate murder. We must as Christ did, love the prostitute even while deploring prostitution.

We must honor always the intent of all man of good purpose. We must respect the honest convictions of all men of good will, even as we condemn the false idea, the unreasoned premise, the twisted logic.

We must not trust passion that is not kept within the realm of ideas, because such a passion must inevitably be on the prowl for human sacrifice.

We know that our greatest mortal enemies are poverty, ignorance, injustice, bigotry, immorality, falsehood, and American Imperialism. We know too that poverty, ignorance, injustice, bigotry, immorality, falsehood, and American Imperialism cannot be shot, cannot be tortured, cannot be fragmented by a bomb.

We must fight them in the labyrinthine maze of our own minds, in the darkest depths of our souls, where they dwell and fester like maggots.

We must fight them with thunderous denunciations, with scintillating shafts of sarcasm, with derision and delicious irony, with calculated insults, with eloquence, laughter, wit and humor --- these are the weapons of the angels against which no evil can prevail.

But never, never with a bullet at the back of the head.

My American friends and their little brown brothers, as well as Jimmy Ongpin, Bernie Villegas, Christian Monsod, Dickie Romulo -- Bosworth, Kaplan, Garrett, Holmes, Croghan --- Jojo Binay, Vic Lim, Blas Ople, Bono Adaza, Johnny Ponce Enrile, Ed Sazon --- should know by now that when I denounce them or make fun of them, I do so not in malice and hatred, but in puckish mischief.

They should know too that in the final analysis, all I really want is to expunge our colonial mentality and our Oedipus Complex towards Mother America ... and to get rid of the "Special Relationship" between the Philippines and the

United States that started long ago when the first American rascal met the first Filipino fool.
June 1, 1987, Philippine Daily Inquirer

Part 6. Christian Monsod, The Raging Bull

Dark of skin, with bulging eyes and an eagle's beak, Christian Monsod looks like a sawed-off version of Tommy Hearns, former welterweight champion of the world. That is why he imagines himself The Raging Bull of the ConCom, and challenges his opponents to a boxing match.

When Commissioner Willie Villacorta questioned Christian about the unseemly haste with which the Four Horsemen (Monsod, Villegas, Bengson, Romulo) were riding roughshod over the nationalist proposals, Christian shouted "What do you mean by that?" And moved to commit mayhem on the poor fellow, with his own friends holding him back of course.

When Commissioner Lino Brocka questioned the fact that some ConCom members had close connections with American Multinational corporations, Christian bellowed, "Are you referring to me?" And moved to decimate him, held back again by Bernie, Peps and Dick.

In an argument with nationalist economist Alejandro Lichauco, Christian turned bullish, shouted an expletive "Cow dung!" or equivalent, and moved to assault Ding. It is a good thing he did not, because Ding just happens to be the Flyweight Champion of Harvard in his time, and would have flattened him out without difficulty.

Nonetheless, it is a sight to see -- Christian Monsod, the Raging Bull, challenging to a trial by arms, nationalists like Commissioners Fely Aquino, Minda Luz Quesada, Rosario Braid, Julie Amargo, and others in his peer class.

Well, the only way to revert the ConCom from a Bull Ring back to a constitutional body is to keep Christian the Raging Bull in check. Christian acts like a Raging Bull only when his Holy Cow, Winnie Monsod, is not around. When she appears anywhere within a mile of him, Christian is instantly transformed to a domesticated ox, and lapses into mute hypnotic stupor.

In Dasmarinas Village, whenever Winnie starts a fight with her husband Christian, all the neighbors rush to their house on Morado Street to bet how many seconds Christian can survive Winnie's left hook.

Christian makes a lot of money selling advertising space on the soles of his shoes, because approximately 20 seconds after the first round, Winnie usually lays Christian on his back. And all the five hours that Christian is unconscious, including the 30 minute trip through traffic to Makati Medical stretched out at the back of a jeepney, the soles of his shoes hanging out of the vehicle, clearly display for all to see, the sterling virtues of Colgate's Toothpaste with Flouride.

For obvious reasons, Christian prefers the more gentle company of Bernie Villegas who would not hurt a flea, though he doth commit murder on the Philippine economy and the English language.

Bernie and Soc Rodrigo appeared in Julie Daza's TV show, to argue the case of the Pro-American Bloc against nationalists Willie Villacorta and Lino Brocka. By God, this Bernie can be so insufferably patronizing. As usual he proceeds from the unreasoned premise that there is a conflict between the Consumer and the Producer. Within the Economy all of us 54 million Filipinos are consumers. Among us consumers, there are those who produce and those who do not produce.

In all his life, Bernie has never produced a single marketable pin or a child, all he did was to serve in the boards of American companies and spout pro-American sentiments. He is seen more in the company of Dick Holmes than in the more pleasant and productive company of Filipina women. Bernie who consumes but does not produce, is an economic parasite. And it should be the proper policy of government to encourage those who produce to produce more, and those who do not produce (like Bernie) to start producing.

Seriously now, Christian and his friends believe that Filipino producers must compete on an equal basis with imported goods and American corporations, in our own domestic market. If we cannot compete "fairly," Christian says, then we deserve to be driven out of business.

Americans reserve the right by "unfair quota limits" to protect General Motors from Toyota, Harley-Davidson motorbikes from Honda, even their sugar beets from our sugar producers ... but Christian would constitutionally guarantee that no such protection will ever be available to the Filipino.

If Christian and his friends really feel that they are the referees between the Filipino and the foreigner, then they should work for the IMF or the World Bank. They have no business being in the payroll of the Filipino people.

Christian and friends are paid to be partisan. They are not referees, they are part of our team, and as such they are paid to promote and protect and defend the interest of the Filipinos against the interests of foreigners ... in the same way that Bosworth and Dick Holmes are paid to promote, protect and defend the interests of the Americans.

I asked Ding Lichauco why he walked away when the Raging Bull made a move to attack him, and he answered, "I don't mind frontally locking horns with the Raging Bull, Larry, but I do mind if he turns around, points his behind at me, and gives me the usual Bullshit!"
September 1, 1986, Philippine Daily Inquirer

Part 7. Christian Monsod was never from Wharton

LETTY G. de Padua is a champion bridge player, with two children who are American citizens -- a widow who is a good friend of Christian Monsod and his wife Winnie.

As may be expected, Winnie and Letty are twin souls, with very strong views and strong ways of expressing them, more like marine sergeants than genteel ladies of a sewing circle. The soft-spoken Christian looks harassed.

I will not quarrel with a widow. But I am afraid Letty's protectiveness toward Christian may have blinded her to certain facts, which I must in conscience point out to her and Christian.

First, I never said Christian's bar exam grade was 80 percent, I said mid-80s.

Second, while Wharton School of Business (not Economics) is in the University of Pennsylvania, Christian Monsod was perhaps kidding about being a graduate of Wharton, he is of the lesser known University of Pennsylvania.

Thirdly, my son Atom is not from Wharton, nor did I ever say so. He is from Harvard Business School. Letty should know, because he is married to her niece, and is her neighbor.

Fourth, I concede that beauty is in the eyes of the beholder, that in the eyes of his wife's best friend, Christian may be assumed to be good-looking, even sexy, as I may be assumed to look like Frankenstein's Monster.

Fifth, I was one of those who recommended Winnie to the NEDA, in preference to Noel Soriano whom I thought was too subservient to Jimmy Ongpin. The National Economic Council which I headed is better than NEDA, being a constitutional body independent of the executive branch, with half the council represented by the Senate and the House, and a fourth by the private sector. NEDA is a mere extension of presidential power. I do not consider myself a rival of Winnie.

Sixth, I do not consider myself anti-American, anymore than Ramsey Clark (an ex-cabinet member here in Manila today) and millions of Americans in the USA who oppose American foreign policy and CIA plots against other nations.

Seventh, I am not against all American corporations, only those who exploit us. I do not consider Atom or those working for American corporations as pro-American. Nor do I consider Americans earning their living here as pro-Filipino.

Eighth, I am not called upon to be grateful to Americans like Phil Kaplan for my son's or my American education, any more than Jose Rizal was grateful to the Spanish friars for having been educated in Madrid. Brains, not the likes of Kaplan, got us into those excellent schools. On the other hand, six wild horses could not get that idiot Kaplan through the portals of Harvard or MIT.

When the Spaniards called Rizal an "ungrateful son", as Letty and Christian call today's American-educated nationalistic Filipinos, Rizal replied:

"If they take us for ingrates, we will be so bold as to reply to them face to face that if, in exchange for the education they give, they require from us that we forswear the truth and the voice of our conscience -- that we stifle the cries of that something God has put within our breasts -- and that we suppress our sense of justice in order to sacrifice to their opulent interests, the interests of our native country, our fellowmen and our brothers -- then we curse and repudiate their education, and let them never expect from us the least measure of gratitude."

Among Rizal's contemporaries, there were those who collaborated with the Spaniards, and those who like Rizal, took the offensive openly, defiantly, courageously with intellectual controversy and even physical combat.

There was Antonio Luna who sought out an arrogant Spanish journalist in a Madrid cafe, and in his own words, "asked him who he was, for I did not know him, called him a despicable coward, spat in his face and threw him my card ... In this way I believe I can show that we Filipinos have more dignity, courage and honor than this cringing and insulting coward who has crossed our path. I think I satisfied our outraged honor."

Now Letty wants to know why I think Christian Monsod is not qualified to be UP president.

(1) Simply because like Jimmy Ongpin, when he is in power, he is intolerant and abusive towards anyone critical of the Americans, towards those who disagree with him. He just won't listen, he won't argue, he won't debate, he just puts on blinders and ear plugs.

In the ConCom, he arrogantly ignored, denigrated, bullied, insulted and challenged to a fight Ding Lichauco, Willie Villacorta and other nationalists. He pointedly turned his back to me, while fawning over Dick Holmes of the Embassy.

In the Namfrel, he insulted Mike Lorza and his Abacus electoral system while kowtowing to Allen Weinstein, a suspected CIA agent peddling a multi million dollar mainframe system. He hints that nationalist leftists are out to sabotage the polls, while ignoring Comelec abuses on Maita Gomez, Bobbit Sanchez, Lean Alejandro and PnB candidates.

Christian Monsod fanatically supports American bases and nuclear bomb storage, IMF policy to revert us to subsistence agriculture, and American domination of our economy.

As UP president, he is apt to curtail academic freedom and have our students setting up barricades and burning his effigy!

(2) Personally I feel that Christian Monsod should work for the IMF and the Americans. He was reportedly to replace Alfredo Velayo as chairman of the Interbank, even as the

American Express was buying 40 percent of it. But the Americans really made a big stink about retaining Fred Velayo. Better Fred than dead, Amex insisted.

Christian was not with GenBank, but he was with ill-fated FilCapital Development, the ill-fated CineManila, the ill-fated Landoil and Pacorp, and the ill-fated Guevent, the ill-fated DMG (assembler of Volkswagen), the ill-fated Radiowealth.

As pointed out by Vicente Albano Pacis, he was in the World Bank in a minor position like other Filipinos who got good positions in Philippine banks. Christian never did.

The only funds Christian can raise for UP would probably come from the CIA.

May 27, 1987, Philippine Daily Inquirer

Part 8. Small Dick's client grows fat on our bones

THE trouble with technocrats, both Marcos' and Cory's, is that they are arrogant and self-righteous; and they assume they know more than we do what is good for us.

Worse, they are congenital pro-Americans, ever on the look-out for a good business connection, a paying client, a job in a multinational or an international agency -- and demeaning the rest of us by constant kowtowing to every neanderthal American in sight.

This column is hard on the Four Horsemen of the ConCom because all Bernie Villegas, Christian Monsod, Peps Bengzon and Dick Romulo ever did was to advance in our Constitution, provisions favoring American bases and its nuclear stockpile, multinational corporations, and the IMF policy to perpetuate a colonial type of plantation economy.

This column is hard on the Council of Trent because such technocrats as Jobo Fernandez, the late Jaime Ongpin and Solita Monsod -- like Cesar Virata, Vicente Valdepenas, Jaime Laya, and Gerardo Sicat -- are committed to enforcing the IMF excremental policy to prevent our industrialization; to shift the tax burden from foreigners to Filipinos and from rich to poor; to impose free trade and import liberalization, and an economy based on export-oriented subsistence agriculture that is labor-intensive, small scale, and rural.

Face it, these technocrats most of whom are only hired help, will never be on the side of the Filipinos. Never.

"Attorney Romulo," asked Dr. Vicenta Escobar of Small Dick, "Just exactly where does your obligation to your client end, and your loyalty to your country begin?"

Small Dick answered that the interest of his client Philippine Geothermal Inc. (PGI), coincides with that of the Philippines, speaking of the contract signed between the two. Yeah? Read on.

The PGI is a 100 percent subsidiary of a US company, Union Oil of California, incorporated July 27, 1971 in California, with an authorized capital of only $500,000 (500 shares at $1,000).

By Sept. 10, 1971, less than two months after its incorporation, and before it got a certification from its own board to qualify as a branch in the Philippines, Dick's client managed to get a service contract with the National Power (NPC) to develop the geothermal resources in Tiwi, Albay, with an area of 17,661 hectares as per Proclamation No. 739, Aug. 14, 1970.

- Dick's client had only eight year's experience in geothermal development previous to its service contract.
- The contract was for a term of 25 years, renewable for another 25 years SOLELY at the option of Dick's client.
- Plans were to set up a 660 MW steam plant in Tiwi and MacBan; only 330 MW were installed.
- The price at which Dick's client supplies steam to the NPC is pegged to the international price of petroleum oil, even if steam is not in any way dependent on oil. This means that as the price of oil inevitably rises (by 2000 AD, the world's reserves will have been depleted), the price of our geothermal power rises proportionately, thus frustrating the promise of cheap geothermal power, to satisfy the greed of Dick's client.
- With a capital of only half a million dollars, Dick's client borrowed not less than $90 million from NPC.
- In 1981, Dick's client ranked no. 82 in gross revenues (P399 million) and 8th in profits (P120 million). In 1985, Dick's client ranked 55th with net sales of P899 million and net income of P495 million. All out of an authorized capital of some P3.5 million, a return that year of 14,142 percent on authorized investment.
- While Tiwi is supplying power to the Manila area, the people

of Tiwi are paying more for their electricity than Manilans do.

Boy, it sure is nice to be Small Dick's American client when Dick's father was in the cabinet and anything nice and nasty can be concocted secretly in the boardrooms of the NPC!

According to Dr. Ting Escobar, the technology employed is defective. Underground water is a non-renewable resource and even now is already drying up in Tiwi, diminishing steam generation, eventually wasting installed capacity.

Studies show that the underground water should have been injected back and not thrown -- such that the squandered hot water caused havoc on land and sea where it was eventually run off.

Small Dick Romulo is wrong when he claims his client's gain is not our country's loss. Only one thing for our legislators to do: NATIONALIZE it!   *April 14, 1988*

Part 9. Till next MBC survey, no more Small Dick

ON September 3, 1986, stung by news stories that branded him, Bernie Villegas, Christian Monsod and Peps Bengzon, "moles for multinationals" and my unrelenting cat-calls naming them the Four Horsemen (War, Death, Plague, Famine) of the ConCom, Commissioner Ricardo J. Romulo stood up to make a privilege speech:

It is alleged that because my law firm represents some foreign investors, I should abstain from voting on provisions in the Article on National Economy and Patrimony.

The proposition advanced, carried to its logical extreme, would apply to any Commissioner here who represents a particular sector. I could ask Bishop Bacani, for example, whether foreigners confess to him, because that may influence him. Or I may ask Commissioner Bernas, whose Jesuit Order is truly multinational, whether that affects him because, unlike me, he takes a vow of obedience.

Several of my Filipino and foreign clients will be affected by the trade liberalization policies of the government. Nevertheless, I voted against "constitutionalizing" protectionism of local industries. Since I represent Lepanto Consolidated Mining Company, a Filipino corporation, I should have voted for a higher percentage of Filipino equity in the natural resources provision; but I did not do so. Again, I should have voted against the 1,000-hectare limitation because I have Filipino clients who will be much affected by that limitation; but instead, I voted for it.

The list of my clients comes from Martindale-Hubbell Law Directory, and none are in natural resources or public utilities. My law firm is more than 25 years old, founded by the late Justice Roman Ozaeta. And in our roster of clients, the ratio is 10 to 1 in favor of Filipino clients.

Of the 34 clients mentioned, 16 were either clients for a single transaction, or no longer operating here or are dormant corporations: American Can, American Smelting and Refinery; Kristian Jebsens; EE Black, Beecham Group Ltd.; Credit Suisse; Dibrell Carolina; Falconbridge Phil.; Granexport; GTE Industries; Mission Exploration; NDC-Guthrie; Reader's Digest; Sime Darby; 20th Century Fox; and Ford Philippines -- which do not even operate here.

My firm's active foreign clients are: Ace-Compton, AHS Philippines, Avon, Coca Cola Export, Cyanamid, Honda, IBM, Mellon Bank; Goulds Pumps, Citibank, Geothermal Philippines, and WR Grace -- none of them in the natural resources or public utilities. The rest are Filipino companies, namely: Hooven-Comalco, Lepanto, National Development Corporation, Philippine Acetylene, Staedler Philippines, Mercury Group and Peter Paul.

I offer Commissioner Bengzon some of my clients so that he can be a bonafide member of the "Four Horsemen."

In Ateneo, reductio-ad-absurdum and non-sequitur are considered more rhetoric than logic. Small Dick can prattle about how many more Filipino clients than American clients he has, but he does not ever mention how much more he earns serving the Americans than he earns serving his countrymen. It is absurd to say that having an itsy bitsy Filipino clients, he serves a greater good by voting for the American interests.

But this is reconciliation day and I turn this column to Gerry Geronimo, Dick's associate whom I respect as a labor lawyer.

o *Regarding our client Philippine Geothermal, though it is true that originally the payment to them is tied to the oil price, it is no longer since 1975 when the reimbursement of investment was based on the US export price index, and the service fee of longer duration is pegged to the US wholesale price index -- not disadvantageous to our country.*

o Do not lump our firm with others who lawyered for Marcos cronies. There is not a single Marcos crony in our list of clients. In the critical years after the August 21 assassination, we in the Romulo office spent more time in rallies and marches than attending to the needs of our clients.

o You harp on Dick's views in ConCom you disagree with, but you ignore the provisions he sponsored which enhanced the independence of the judiciary, institutionalized people power through initiative and referendum, and other pro-people provisions.

Okay, okay, till the next MBC survey which I expect to be even worse than the last one, we shall write no more Small Dick.

September 13, 1988, Philippine Daily Inquirer

Part 10. Orbos worth two million, Starke two cents

EVERYBODY knows why Father Kinik Bernas' Ateneo Survey denigrated the only real democratic institution, the independent Legislature, especially the Senate, as having lost the confidence of the people. Instead Bernas' Survey highlighted public approbation of the military over the civilian, of General Fidel Ramos over President Cory Aquino. Also, Opus Dei CRC conducted a survey indicating the preference of big businessmen for a dictatorial military junta over a representative democracy.

The Ateneo and Opus Dei CRC surveys reflect the concern of the American government over the fate of the Bases in the Philippines. Father Kinik Bernas and the CRC, sympathizers of Americans, are testing the waters for the abolition of the Senate, the main obstacle to the ratification of the future Bases Agreement, and the possibility of a coup d'etat and a military junta to accomplish the American goal.

Now that the House has proven to be more malleable than the Senate, and easily corruptible, the Americans are happy that Sen. Edong Angara is sponsoring a constitutional amendment to change the legislature from bicameral to unicameral.

In the Constitutional Commission, the bicameral form

was adopted by a plurality of only one vote. The unicameral chamber was once universally preferred because it was ideal for the parliamentary form deemed more responsive to the people's mandate.

But Dick Holmes, the CIA agent considered the 49th member of the ConCom, was not sure this suited America's interest. A Prime Minister who is replaceable at any time cannot be depended upon to act consistently in America's best interests. Moreover, a unicameral body is larger and harder to control than 24 members of the Senate.

The history of the pre-Marcos senate indicate that notwithstanding the presence of the Great Nationalists Laurel, Recto and Diokno, there are more of Cabili, Primicias, Osias and Arneooo Boys to insure that America's interest is amply protected and advanced.

In the 1986 ConCom, Dick Holmes did not give clear instructions to the Four Horsemen, Esperanza Club and that pro-American jackass Blas Ople. The vote was close, but to the credit of First Secretary Dick Holmes and his bosses, Ambassador Steve Bosworth and Minister Dave Kaplan, the Americans got what they wanted -- a bicameral presidential form of government for us Flips.

But the best laid plans of mice and men often go awry (pronounced *aray*, as in Ouch). A concerted effort was made to ease out the Nationalists and Independents from the cabinet -- Bobbit Sanchez, Joker Arroyo, Rene Saguisag, Bert Romulo, Tito Guingona, Letty Shahani, Jovy Salonga, Monching Mitra, Neptali Gonzales -- most of whom asked to run for public office in 1987. They were replaced by vacuum-weights and non-entities beholden to the Council of Trent, Makati Business Club and the Americans.

Namfrel and Comelec were markedly pro-American, associated with "Center for Democracy" headed by suspected CIA agent Allen Weinstein.   And there were enough oppositionists like Juan Ponce Enrile, Kit Tatad, Lorenz Teves to insure a pro-American Senate, especially with Father Bernas' pro-American Ateneo Social Weather Station predicting that at least ten opposition senators will be elected.

The Americans simply miscalculated.   Most voters today are born without an umbilical cord to the colonial past, and are the only generation that has never known what it is to be under a foreign master. After elections, we had a nationalistic Senate, including Juan Ponce Enrile and Joseph Estrada.

Now the lackeys of Americans want to abolish the Senate, in favor of a unicameral body mostly composed of those in the House.

With all due respect to Monching Mitra and my friends in the House, one Senator has more brains and sense of nationalism than half of the House put together. The so-called Representatives who cannot even give us a decent and effective Land Reform, who buckle before every pressure from the military, Council of Trent and Malacañang, who are the villains in every major scandal from the importation of UZIs to buko quotas to unconscionable junketeering and influence peddling -- actually voted themselves P17,000 salary and allowances of P65,000 a month or a total of P1 million a year each.

Are they really worth all that money? Well, Mon Mitra, Oscar Orbos, Boni Gillego, Raul Daza, Raul Roco, Joe de Venecia, Lorna Verano-Yap and Nikki Coseteng are worth more than twice that amount. Hortense Starke and Jose Ong are worth two cents. And presidential relatives are worth one million bucks each, as long as they can be persuaded not to attend the sessions.

Let's abolish the House instead of the Senate.
March 13, 1989, Philippine Daily Inquirer

Part 11. Nationalist Azcuna deflected Monsod's thrust

UNDER Supreme Commander Douglas MacArthur, Japan adopted a constitution renouncing war as an instrument of national policy. It was the best thing that ever happened, for it allowed Japan to concentrate on economic development inspite of American efforts to get Japan to arm itself against America's enemies.

The provision in our constitution for a no-nukes policy was intended to accomplish the same result. It was in effect a commitment to world peace, and a step towards making the ASEAN region a zone of peace, freedom and neutrality.

Dick Holmes, CIA agent and "49th member" of the ConCom did not agree, and neither did his colleague Christian Monsod, who together with Small Dick Romulo, Bernie

"Alopecic Gynander" Villegas, and Peps "Little Brown Jug-ears" Bengzon consistently voted to promote American interest in the ConCom.

The four were tagged "Four Horsemen of the ConCom" in reference to the Bible's Horsemen of the Apocalypse: Famine (on a white horse), War (red), Pestilence (black) and Death (pale). Because of his pigmentation Christian "Boy" Monsod assumed the role of Pestilence.

During the ConCom sessions of October 7-8, 1986, Boy Monsod moved for the reconsideration of the approval of Section 7 which read, "The Philippines, consistent with the national interest, adopts and pursues a policy of freedom from nuclear weapons in its territory."

As suggested by Holmes, Boy Monsod proposed an amendment that would change the phrase, "consistent with" to "subject to."

The Magnificent Dozen who were nationalists, knew that with the pressure being exerted by the US embassy, Boy's pro-American amendment might just pass. And if it did, Boy might be encouraged by Dick Holmes, Minister Pssst Kaplan and US Ambassador Steve Bosworth, to go on an orgy of amendments to purge the constitution of its nationalistic provisions.

Under Boy Monsod's relentless questioning, Adolfo Azcuna of the nationalist bloc, admitted that the phrase "consistent with" was meant to mean "subject to." It was a deliberate ploy on the part of the nationalists to avoid a vote on Monsod's amendment.

When Commissioner Jamir maintained that the meaning remains doubtful, Monsod demanded that if the meaning is unclear, his pro-American motion be submitted to a vote.

The nationalist bloc thought it was the better part of valor not to challenge the might of the CIA, and settled for co-sponsoring a resolution saying it is "the intent and sense" of the ConCom that the term "consistent with" means also "subject to." The resolution was passed unanimously.

It is the contention of pro-American Boy Monsod that since the ConCom voted to interpret the phrase "consistent with national interest" as allowing nuclear arms in the bases if national interest so dictates.

On the other hand, it is the contention of many Filipinos that they voted for the Constitution, not for Boy Monsod's Resolution. Most of them did not bother to look over the records, as Jamir warned. They voted for the wording of the constitution, whose meaning is clear and straightforward to people who speak English: the no-nukes policy IS consistent with national policy, and any other interpretation is a strained twisting of the English language.

Fortunately, the final interpretation of any constitutional provision lies ultimately in the hands of the Supreme Court.

The Supreme Court tries to divine the thinking of the people when they voted for the constitution. Is the language clear in its meaning? At this point the Court disregards the minutes of the sessions and the resolution of Boy Monsod.

If the Court decides that the meaning is not clear, then the justices will look into the records of the constitution, and consult experts of the English language. What do the words "consistent with" mean when read by the common people? Does it mean "subject to" or "in consonance with"?

"Consistent with my nationalism, I object to the presence of the bases" -- does it mean "unless dictated otherwise by my sense of nationalism" or does it mean "in consonance with my nationalism"?

"Consistent with national interest, there should be no nuclear arms in the bases" -- does it mean "unless dictated by national interest"? -- in which case, it implies that no-nukes may be against national policy!

Only "Uncle Tom" Chris Monsod n his cotton-picking mind, would think so.

July 22, 1988, Philippine Daily Inquirer

Part 12. Aunt Teresa protests; vigilantes go berserk!

MY wife's aunt, Ma. Teresa F. Nieva, former ConCom delegate, now Executive Director of the Bishops-Businessmen's Conference for Human Development (BBC), protests my allegation that the BBC is among the hawk organizations bent on imposing Singlaub's LIC bloodbath on us.

She wrote: "For the record, we would like to state that the BBC has neither endorsed nor advocated the LIC. It is inaccurate and unfair for Mr. Henares to ascribe a position to

BBC that has no basis in fact."

Neither did BBC ever condemn the LIC bloodbath, as did many religious organizations concerned about the assassination of nationalists and priests.

These religious organizations are smeared by militarists as "communist fronts" -- a tactic BBC did not condemn either.

Auntie Teresa continues: "On the contrary, BBC has always stood for solutions to the insurgency that strike at the roots of the problem. That is why BBC has been in the forefront of consultations and forums all over the country, even during Mr. Marcos' regime, dealing with human and civil rights, Basic Christian Communities, industrial peace, people's participation in decision-making processes, etc."

Ha, ha, I did not see Atty. Ricardo Romulo in MABINI or FLAG engaged in the struggle for human rights; he was busy representing his 40 foreign clients.

Ha, ha, I did not see Bishop Ted Bacani overly active in Sister Mariani Dimaranan's Task Force Detainees.

Ha, ha, I did not see the BBC protest when suspected CIA agent Russ Munro condemned the Basic Christian Communities as communist organizations. Not a peep from Auntie Teresa.

Ha, ha, industrial peace indeed! -- BBC members were in the forefront of the campaign to de-stabilize the labor movement, by conspiring against Secretary of Labor Bobbit Sanchez, Jimmy Tadeo and the KMU.

Ha, ha, -- the people's participation in the decision-making process -- how, by holding conferences between bishops and businessmen? A morning daily reported that BBC is more of a businessmen's organization than anything else.

Concluded Auntie Teresa: "BBC advocates a comprehensive agrarian reform program, urban land reform and social housing, and other social justice measures. It has conducted para-legal workshops for the urban poor, one of many similar programs in line with its commitment to justice and liberation for total human development."

Their land reform is patterned after that of suspected CIA agent Roy Prosterman in Vietnam, Guatemala and El Salvador -- an anti-insurgency measure designed to frustrate industrialization.

The Catholic Church is undergoing a schism between progressive elements committed to Liberation Theology, nationalism and preferential option for the poor ... and conservative elements dedicated to the perpetuation of American Imperialism and the intolerable status quo.

I have seen the co-chairman of BBC, leading an electoral watchdog organization that is financed by the American meddlers (as recounted on pages 407 to 410 of Raymond Bonner's Waltzing with a Dictator).

I have seen the same man, as a ConCom delegate along with Auntie Teresa Nieva (Executive Director), Small Dick Romulo and Bishop Teodoro Bacani (both in the BBC Executive Committee), actually sponsor the right of Americans to establish military bases here, institutionalize IMF policy limiting our development to export-oriented agriculture, not full industrialization, and support the right of Americans to store nuclear weapons in the Philippines -- precipitating a mass walkout of nationalists.

His close colleague Bernardo Villegas, in the ConCom is a member of a religious organization that collaborated with the CIA in Chile to overthrow and murder Salvador Allende -- an organization devoted to love of luxury and disdain for the poor, training poor Filipinas how to be good servants to the rich.

I have seen the Honorary Co-Chairman of BBC actually refer to nationalists opposed to American bases and American monopolies, as "lepers" to be shunned and denied their right to participate in democratic elections.

For condemning vigilante death squads, American Imperialism, and violation of human rights -- the Association of Major Religious Superiors, Task Forces Detainees, Socio-Pastoral Institute, Ecumenical Council, PAHRA, Rural Missionaries of the Philippines, GABRIELA of Sister Mary John Mananzan, have been branded as Communist Fronts.

Can we assume that church organizations with opposite views are by the same token, CIA Fronts??

On Nov. 26, a right-wing paper reported five people were killed and seven others were wounded when three alleged members of a vigilante group in Cebu called "Bantay Silangan" went on a killing spree.

The gunmen with M-16 Armalites first shot two persons in a rattan factory, then went into a store nearby and mowed down two others. Then faced a group of gamblers and shot four. Finally they marched up to a house and killed two drinking friends.

These unsavory characters are the type that gravitate towards CIA-sponsored death squads -- gunning for those who oppose American bases and American monopolies, and for priests and doctors with preferential option for the poor.

They are the type that ambushed with treachery and superior force: Ninoy Aquino, Lean Alejandro, Lando Olalia, the brother of Crispin Beltran, and Nemesio Prudente ... with impunity because the police never get to apprehend them.

Who are these vigilantes?

Trigger-happy scoundrels with grudges and personal scores to settle ... ex-communists with a yen to continue their violent way of life ... communists and fellow travelers who find in vigilantism an appropriate cover for their activities ... fanatics of all sorts -- with gun permits easy to come by from a sympathetic military, in spite "guidelines" -- abound in vigilante organizations.

God, these are organizations that escape condemnation from the BBC and Auntie Teresa.

December29, 1987, Philippine Daily Inquirer

Part 13. Nobody believed Montesquieu, so why me?

DELIGHTED to receive accolades (PDI, Aug. 7) from Antonio O. Decolongon whom I have never met, but whom I long admired for one act of principle.

The night Wellington "Willie" Koo Jr., a Stonehill associate, was awarded by the Business Writers Association (BWAP) for pioneering in mutual funds 25 years ago, Willie left early to celebrate at Bayside Night Club.

Whereupon, the story goes, his public relations man, Tony Decolongon, said, "I can not abide having to sing praises about one so unworthy of being a good example to our youth. I quit." Long after, the act of Tony lingered in our memory.

Tony is the brother of radio announcer Ray Oliver who used their mother's family name, dropping Decolongon because it was hard to pronounce.

Tony is happily married to an Australian girl for many years now, is now in the export business.

Thanks, Tony.

Secretary Eddie Ramos called me up in anger and anguish: "I thought we were friends and god-brothers. How could you do this to me? Linking my name to Nikki Coseteng! You can joke with me in private, Larry, but not in public. Some people believe what you write!"

I often make fun of those I like, but this was no joke. Nikki told me of the whispering campaign against her by the CIA.

"Larry, *itong bulong-bulong sobra na.* Expose it in print so that people can see how ridiculous it is! My friend Fely said that from the highest source came gossip linking me with Eddie Ramos.   That's slanderous, no man who favors American bases can get to within a mile of me, you know that. Eddie is out."

I apologize.   Sorry I mentioned Eddie since he is sensitive about it, especially since a dozen guys in Congress resent being left out by the CIA. I wouldn't mind being gossiped about in the same way. My wife won't believe it, but if Christian and Small Dick believed it and envied me, I'd be in seventh heaven.

When I am in a mood for humor, I am guided by Charles Louis de Secondat, Baron de la Berde et de Montesquieu (1689-1755), famed French philosophical historian, who once wrote: "I wouldn't be half so bold if it were my lot to be believed."

Ordinarily I wouldn't defend cousin Peps Bengzon, little brown jug-ears who was the Fourth Horseman of the ConCom. But Peps was unfairly accused by the PCGG as a Kokoy dummy along with Cory's *bayaw* Baby Lopa and Andres Siochi.

Ridiculous! The truth:

- First Manila Management Corp. (FMMC), organized by the Cojuangco, Lopa and Siochi in 1967, was sold to Kokoy Romualdez in 1974 for only P1.01 million.
- The personal guarantees of the former owners over the firm's multimillion pesos liabilities were to be extinguished, but were not.

- To protect themselves, the former owners designated Atty. Peps Bengzon as legal counsel. As a result the guarantees were never called.
- It was a common assumption among the managers that the FMMC group will be returned to the rightful owners after the Marcos era. One day after the revolution, the officers and employees negotiated with Kokoy.
- Lopa and Siochi agreed to buy back their minority share of the firm while the Cojuangco family declined and waived their rights in favor of FMMC's officers and employees.
- PCGG sequestered the shares which Joaquin Cunanan & Co. re-evaluated at P5 million.
- Peps Bengzon and partners were lawyers concerned with the extinction of personal guarantees of the former owners, later with collection and foreclosure, never in management. They were trusted by Cojuangco and Lopa.
- Peps' law partners including Adolfo Azcuna, acted as incorporators of the FMMC companies, and endorsed the shares in blank to the authorized FMMC representative. Neither Peps Bengzon nor Rep. Isidro Zarraga were incorporators.
- The 6.3 million PCIB shares were bought from First Philippine Holdings at higher than market price, with the beneficial ownership of Kokoy formally disclosed to PCGG by partner Eriberto Narciso. The Soloil borrowed to pay for the shares, and keeps the shares because the PCGG never asked for them.
- The P20 million "donation" was based on a compromise idea that receivables from collected from Trans Middle East be ceded directly to the Philippine Treasury. To depict it as bribery is uncalled for.

All these were deliberately distorted by PCGG to show that the Kokoy divestment is fictitious and that Cory's family and Peps are dummies of Kokoy. That is really dung.

August 13, 1988, Philippine Daily Inquirer

Part 14. JoeCon is a dog, a pit bull terrier

JOECON the Immaculate Misconception, Secretary of Trade & Industry, achieved his successes so far because he has the mentality of a pit bull terrier. Once he has his eyes set on a particular objective, he charges forward without fear or caution or reason, blinders on, right or wrong, unswerving, unstoppable.

A pit bull terrier has nothing but dogged determination. Once his jaws close in on something, he never lets go even unto death. Boiling water, a knife at the throat, even a bullet in the brain have often failed to unclench the lock-jaw bite.

That is why JoeCon does so well manning political movements where limited knowledge and intelligence, canine loyalty and bulldog fanaticism are at a premium -- the Pasay Citizen's Council for Good Government, Namfrel, and Bishop-Businessmen's Conference.

This pit bull terrier mentality has also made JoeCon the champion patsy and all-day sucker for scheming villains who manage to get JoeCon to do their dirty work for them, and to get the blame for their ill-doing.

- JoeCon is patsy for Our Man Squint Buenaventura and the Luzon Petroleum Company (LPC), for championing whose behest loans and transfer to Batangas, JoeCon is now being crucified by the press.

- For that matter he is the patsy of his brother Raul, and his son Jose III, whose businesses come within the purview of his cabinet portfolio, and because of whom he is now being investigated by Congress.

- JoeCon is a patsy for his deputy Tom Alcantara who lets JoeCon promote his favorite foreigners (Taiwanese and Koreans), and his own cement interests.

- And also a patsy for a beleaguered Cory administration longing to fulfill an Impossible Dream, screaming meaningless slogans divorced from reality -- Philippines, an NIC by 2000 AD! -- Yes we can! -- and claiming a flood of foreign investments that are belied by Central Bank figures.

- JoeCon is also a patsy for the Technocrats who grabbed the Iligan Steel from the Jacintos in order to frustrate the integration of the steel industry. After he took over from Bobby Ongpin, after a conference with Cesar Virata, he decided to keep Rolly Narciso and the Ongpin technocrats in the National Steel and the Jacintos out of it. In this way he is serving the purposes of the Council of Trent, IMF and the Marcos technocrats.

To discharge this duty, he keeps the truth from Cory and to the nation. He cites the Laya UP Report commissioned by Marcos, repudiated by UP President Jose Abueva and discredited by the Valdellon Report. He cites the Laya Report being confirmed by the COA, which COA Commissioner Eufemio Domingo denies.

In the meantime, the National Steel is being used as a milking cow by the technocrats. President Rolly Narciso drew a bonus of over P300,000.

For Christian Monsod (who once worked at the NDC with JoeCon) and his Container factory, the National Steel imports steel plates and sells them to Christian at a price TWO PERCENT ABOVE COST, practically a give-away and a subsidy.

By keeping National Steel under his technocrats' control, JoeCon also assures a cheap and plentiful supply of black iron sheets for his family's Carrier airconditioning and Kelvinator refrigerator factory, as well as tin-plates and tin-cans for his Swift and RFM food processing plants.

When JoeCon the Immaculate Misconception appeared before Sonny Osmeña's Senate Committee, he reportedly shocked Sonny and the newsmen by saying, *"Baka may kailañgan ka sa departamento ko, Sonny. Kung mayroon, sabihin mo lang, at ako na ang bahala."*

Sonny was absolutely embarrassed at JoeCon's assumption that Sonny is persecuting him in order to gain some political advantage, *"Talagang hindi mawala ang pagka intsik ni JoeCon."*

Sonny is determined to pursue his investigation into the official actions of JoeCon that benefited his family businesses, the loans and accommodations and rulings from government agencies his family companies have taken advantage of, and the various pressures he exerted to favor foreign companies and his friends in the Council of Trent.

While others may backtrack, JoeCon would rush in where angels fear to tread, with the same bulldog tenacity with which he pursued a university degree in the Araneta University.

And so the pit bull terrier JoeCon continues with lockjaw doggedness, to bulldoze his way through life, without rhyme or reason, or regard for national interest, taking up causes thrust upon him by villainous schemers, and totally oblivious of the dire consequences to himself and to the country.

We can only grieve that JoeCon the Immaculate Misconception does not have the mental acuity to realize the need to zig or zag or stop or backtrack to save his foolish ass. *June 2, 1999, Philippine Daily Inquirer*

Part 15. NO wins debates but YES may win in polls

There was a Great Student Debate between Ateneo Law School (affirmative side) and UP Law (negative) on the ratification of the constitution. Debate Chairman Ric Dong Puno said; "None of the debaters won, but the audience did." Oh yeah?

I am more of Ateneo than UP, I vote a critical YES, and I demanded an explanation from my son Danby, an Ateneo Law student: "How in heaven's name did Ateneo take a beating from UP? Atenean Ric Dong Puno was chairman, blast his hide, why didn't he throw stink bombs to disrupt the proceedings and end our humiliation?

"And Danby, you're a good debater. You could have browbeaten those two plebians, and broken the heart of their girl researcher, so why the hell were you not there defending the Blue Eagle? No cokes this week, Daniel, I just lost your allowance in a bet with your uncle Ding Lichauco."

Danby answered; "Papa, with so much homework, no fourth year student could spare the time. Our debaters are all in Third Year. Olma Inocentes came from UP, and had Roderick Paulate as boyfriend. Michael Tantoco has no girl friend. Our researcher Ben-Hur Olivas, son of General O, is named after the greatest cochero that ever lived. A trio of Nervous Nellies, how could they possibly win??

"Those plebians from UP are upperclassmen, polished in debate, and personally fulfilled. Justin Adviento just became a father. Jose Baylon loves researcher Maria Gabriela Roldan who passed love notes to him during the debate. Those frat brats were in the pink of health and morale. How could they lose??"

We of the YES have been losing debates lately. Three times ConComm Bernardo Villegas (pro) and Alejandro Lichauco (con) debated the merits of the Article 12 of the draft on "National Economy and Patrimony". In such Battle of the Balds, poor Bernie comes out second best, not being used to open, free and fair debate. The disadvantage of a religious fanatic like Bernie is that he has a closed mind, his perception of fact and fiction is blurred because reality is distorted to fit his convictions.

For instance, the Chinese economy had always been 100 percent closed economy, till Deng Xiaoping opened it by 5 percent to allow foreign investment in one export zone --- and Bernie proclaims to the world that China opened its doors and achieved a 12 percent GNP rise. On the other hand, the Philippines had always had a 90 per cent open economy, with open arms for foreign investment --- and Bernie declares that the Philippines is too closed and must open up 100 percent in order to achieve the success of China. In other words, Bernie judges a 95 percent closed China market as OPEN; and a 90 percent open Philippine market as CLOSED. Weird.

Bernie says that the Philippines should abandon industrialization and develop agriculture as did Taiwan and South Korea. Taiwan has 22 percent of its labor force in agriculture, and 42 percent in industry; has a per capita income of $2,143. South Korea has 21.8 percent of its labor in agriculture, 44 percent in industry; and a per capita income of $1,880. The Philippines has 47 percent of its labor force in agriculture, 12 percent in industry; and a per capita of $514 in 1986. How did Bernie imagine that Taiwan and Korea are agricultural and that we Flips had an industrialization program?

This explains why Bernie Villegas keeps losing debates to Ding Lichauco. In Boston, no Harvard boy is ever considered one unless he has an undergraduate degree from Harvard University. Two-year wonders from the Business school are considered interlopers. In this sense, Ding is more of a Harvard man than Bernie claims to be. Ding is from Ateneo, Bernie is from La Salle. Ding is Jesuit-trained, Bernie is encapsulated in Opus Dei. Ding eats balut; Bernie regurgitates balut as a violation of the right to life of the unborn. Oh, my God!

The economic provisions as well as those that allow military bases in the Philippines are an abomination, institutionalizing IMF and American colonial policies in the basic law of the land. Oppositionist Arturo Tolentino knows this, so he lures ConComm Ambrosio Padilla into these issues, and wins amidst applause. At least Sonny Alvarez was able to manuever Tolentino to an inconclusive stand-off.

A critical YES is easier to defend than an unequivocal YES. We should not be trapped into defending the indefensible. Let us concede the abomination of those two provisions and join issues on Social Justice, Judicial Process and People's Power. Then dwell on the system of initiative and referendum, as well as Constituent Assembly by which we can amend the abominable provisions introduced by ConComm Villegas, Romulo, Bengson and Monsod. That is the only way to win the debate.

Tonight on Channel 4, 10-11 pm on "ConCom and You", Transitory Provisions debated by Counsel Rene Saguisag, ex-Governor Aguedo Agbayani, ConComm Rustico de los Reyes. Tune in.

NO may win debates, but my critical YES may still win in the plebiscite. I am betting Danby's next allowance on that.
January 20, 1987

Part 16. Bel tolls for Geny: Curses, foiled again!

WHATEVER happened to the famous adventure comic strip, Hairbreadth Harry, a blonde curly haired hero whose nemesis was a cloaked bemoustached blackguard called Rudolph Rassendale?

Hairbreadth Harry, so called because he specialized in rescuing maidens at the last minute from the brink of a fate worse than death, always manages to frustrate the villain. Rudy in the last frame, always slinks from the scene, ranting behind his cloak, "Curses, foiled again!"

Hairbreadth Larry I may be, but Bel Cunanan deserves a lot of the credit. Ask not, Geny, for whom the Bel tolls; it tolls for thee.

Three times, Geny Lopez was to triumph in his designs, and three times at the brink of success and at the very last minute, he had to slink away, ranting "Curses, foiled again!"

First was the time he wanted to take over People's Television Channel 4. He had every right to it, according to Executive Secretary Joker Arroyo, Presidential Adviser Rene

Saguisag, and Information Secretary Teddyboy Locsin, because when Marcos took over ABS-CBN, he did not bother to transfer the network to some other entity. It remained under the name of the Lopezes, and Malacañang was ready to hand it over sometime in January, 1987.

On the very day the Lopezes were to meet with Asst. Executive Secretary Catalino Macaraig for the formal turnover, I had breakfast with Geny Lopez in his Dasma home along with Jake Almeda Lopez, and we discussed the transfer scheduled for three in the afternoon.

I went back to the Inquirer with a scoop about the turnover of Channel 4, only to find Bel Cunanan agitated because Teddyboy told her about it too. It seems Teddyboy had a change of mind, as he reminded us that his father never got really compensated for the closing of his beloved Free Press. "Some people think patriotism is convertible to cash," said Teddyboy, "If Geny wants Channel 4, let him go to court like everyone should."

Dodie Limcaco came over to complain that Channel 4 was the symbol of the Edsa Revolution, and that many people, including me, risked their lives to capture and protect it. And for whom, the Lopezes??

Bel got to work. That afternoon at the very last minute, Macaraig did not show up, and Geny Lopez slinked away, ranting, "Curses, foiled again!"

The second time around, the Meralco deal, approved by the Committee on Privatization was already being implemented, as the PCGG lifted its sequestration order and the APT took over the Meralco shares. The shares was to be transferred to the Lopez-BPI-Morgan on July 21, 1988.

Someone in Malacañang sent me a copy of the 65-paged project proposal, "Larry, na *approbahan na ito, pero hindi namin na intindihan*. DBP chairman Jess Estanislao fast-talked us into it. *Tingnan no ng*"

I had breakfast again with Geny and his brothers Oscar (FPHI president) and Manolo (Meralco president), and being friends from way back, I told them what I was going to write, "Okay lang, sport lang," they said, knowing that the turnover was soon, and it is too late to stop it.

I wrote a series of articles that ended four days before the deal was concluded, on July 17. On that very same day, headlines screamed that President Cory suspended the deal, and ordered a renegotiation. Instead of getting the deal through at a bargain price of P690 million, the Lopezes will have to shell out to the government 30 percent of the profits, about P2.5 billion.

"Curses, foiled again!"

The third time, last Christmas Eve, the Lopezes succeeded in getting almost all of the lower House to sponsor and pass a bill granting their ABS-CBN a super-franchise, an all-purpose all-encompassing franchise to operate all types of communication facilities, including the authority to receive and transmit messages, impressions, picture, music, and data throughout the country and abroad, as well as ships, aircraft and other conveyances.

Beetle brains in Congress congratulated themselves for the passing of a bill "unprecedented in speed and smoothness," while another admitted, "It was a Merry Christmas bill. Anyway, it will be vetoed."

Well, I wrote about it on January 18, in a satirical piece "Super Franchise: Empire Strikes Back," depicting Geny as Skywalker, and his brothers Oscar and Manolo as R2D2 and C3PO respectively. This was followed by articles written by Bel Cunanan. And today, two months later, the bill is stuck in the Senate, and Malacañang threatens to veto it if it is passed. The Senate assures us it won't.

"Curses, foiled again!" said Rudy Rassendale, as he slinked from the scene, raising his cloak to hide his face and moustache, as Hairbreadth Harry triumphed again.

"Curses, foiled again," said Geny Lopez.

March, 1989, Philippine Daily Inquirer

Part 17. Aliens act like God sitting in Judgment

ANY intelligent self-respecting Filipino resents being tested and evaluated by foreigners, as if they were God sitting in Judgment over the Filipino people. This is a privilege they arrogate to themselves while enjoying our hospitality, but if in turn we pass judgment on them, we are deemed anti-foreign, and therefore damnable.

Filipinos are pretty hard on each other, we criticize each other viciously. I like to believe we do so because we know our virtues and would like to correct our faults. But there is no reason for foreigners to criticize us except to satisfy their white man's vanity.

Every diplomatic official, every alien resident, every 30-day wonder who comes to our shores to write about us, every neanderthal of low IQ, every white trash a week unwashed -- such as Tony Spaeth, Phil Kaplan, Michael Byrne, Erich Geiling, Belgian Ambassador Alain Rens -- feels free privately and publicly to make distinctions between Filipinos who are bad and Filipinos who are good. To make indecent jokes about Cory and other officials. And to pass judgment on the Filipino's deficiencies.

Maybe Small Dick and Uncle Tom take this as the inherent right of a superior race to pass judgment on an inferior one. But I don't. As a Filipino I will criticize aliens who criticize us. I have done it to Americans, Britons, Dutch, Belgians, Italians, Germans, Malaysians, and I am just waiting for the French, the Israelis and the Russians to make their move.

The Japanese, Chinese, Indians and other colored races except the Malaysians (with their British arrogance), are usually good guests who do not abuse our hospitality.

Pero itong mga puti, kala mo kung sino, talagang mayabang. Flips, don't ever let them get away with insulting Filipinos, give it to them tit for tat before it gets to be a habit for them to heap dung on us.

So do yourself a favor, every time you hear a foreigner insult us, every time you type a letter for your foreign boss heaping abuse on Filipinos -- let me know, let me have his name, nationality, what he said, to whom and when. And we will wipe the floor with his butt.

A friend gave me xerox copies of parts of a book "Cockatoo's Handbook Philippines" by Daniel Ludszuweit, 1642 Adriatico, Malate, Manila Tel. 521-2544, in which the author took to task CID Commissioner Miriam Defensor Santiago, General Alfredo Lim, Cardinal Vidal of Cebu, and myself for "anti-foreign paranoia." On the other hand he heaped praises on Sen. Sonny Osmeña for supporting the American bases.

This German cockalorum cockatoo, a parrot with conspicuous erectile crest, lectures us on Nationalism which he says is the tool of such dictators as Napoleon and Hitler, and nothing but "deception, like Religion."

Nationalism carried to excess becomes Imperialism of course, but without Nationalism, we become victims of Colonialism, as we Filipinos have been for centuries. This German ninnylobcock lectures against Nationalism to a colonial people subject to a foreign power -- in effect he is lecturing on the evils of Gluttony to a starving people.

Herr Ludszuweit resents the action of Lady Miriam, General Lim, and Cardinal Vidal in protecting Filipina women from foreign sex deviates, saying that "sexual self-realization for material advantage" is basically legitimate, and is to be found in marriages as well as in prostitution.

Ludszuweit speculates that Lady Miriam Defensor Santiago and I are probably CIA agents, "Miriam and Larry getting information from the CIA, so the two could continue blaming more and more Philippine politicians for being anti-Filipino and maneuver them into an anti-anti-foreign position."

Well, as he passed judgment on us, we claim the right to pass judgment on him -- Daniel Ludszuweit is an ignorant, contemptible nincompoop, a neo-Nazi and an unmitigated ass.

Speaking of Neo-Nazis, Franz Joseph Strauss, head of the Christlich Sociale Union Party in Bavaria, and its financial arm Hans Seidel Stiftung, recently donated $250,000 or P5.34 million to Benardo Villegas to set up an Opus Dei university in the Philippines.

One remembers that Herr Strauss was the Defense Minister under the postwar German Chancellor Konrad Adenaur, but was forced to resign because he authorized a raid on the magazine Der Spriegel. Strauss was known as a neo-Nazi and was also involved in graft and corruption in defense contracts.

Neo-Nazi Strauss and his Hans Seidel Stiftung financed the building of Opus Dei CRC building on Pearl Street in the Ortigas Pasig Complex. When it was inaugurated, Strauss came to the Philippines, presented a gold-plated gun to the dictator Marcos, and stayed as a guest of Malacañang.

Another unmitigated ass.

Date?

Part 18. Needle Dick needles me for being happy

MY kabaleyan Al Mendoza sent me a column by Mike Royko which tells of Grump, the reactionary conservative partisan of CIA Director George Bush. Grump was grumpy because Mike Royko, a liberal Democrat, is not depressed at all at George Bush's election to the US presidency. Which is more or less what happened between Small Dick and myself a few days ago. So this is going to look like paraphrase of Mike Royko.

Small Dick, also known as Needle Dick, an incorrigible pro-American, looked sad and depressed, so I asked what is wrong.

"You should be happy," I said, "After all, the revised Military Agreement has been signed. Undersecretary Fernando Abat, also known as Shorty with his brain too close to his butt, has declared that members of BAYAN, KMU, Gabriela and other cause-oriented groups are communist dupes, and therefore killable by CIA assassins.

"Human Rights Commissioner Mary Concepcion Bautista who looks like the Bride of Frankenstein, says that abuse of human rights are done by everyone except the military. Ateneo and Father Kinik Bernas, Opus Dei and Bernie Villegas are preparing our people for the Military Bases beyond 1992 and a CIA-sponsored military junta. And General Ramos is on his way to be the president of the Philippines.

"You have won, Small Dick, you and the Americans have won. You should be deliriously happy!"

Answered Small Dick, "I am unhappy because you are so damn cheerful, Larry."

Come on, Small Dick, why should I not be cheerful? It's Christmastime, the sun is shining, the birds are singing, and my daughter Rosanna actually kissed me without being asked.

"You lost, you bastard," Small Dick shouted, "You lost and you don't have the common decency to look miserable. You are not sporting enough to admit you are depressed. You are trying to deprive me of the hard-earned joy of seeing you whimper with your tail between your legs."

But Small Dick, I just don't feel bad. I don't have cross-eyes and a badly asymmetrical face. I am accustomed to losing and probably would have gone into shock if the Americans suddenly become humble and respectful towards the Filipino people. And I like General Eddie Ramos, I think he will turn out okay.

"Shithead, are you implying my eyes are crossed and my face not symmetrical? And how dare you say you like Eddie Ramos! You have no right to like him. I forbid you to like him!"

Aw, Small Dick, you should be glad that like Helen of Troy, you have the kind of a face that can launch a nuclear war. And I do like Eddie Ramos. I am not crazy about him, but I know him long enough since we were young to know he suffered racial discrimination in the West Point. I think that unlike his subordinate Shorty, he is basically a political moderate who tends to be humane and liberal in his views.

"Be careful, Henares, you are coming close to being slanderous and libelous. You have no right to call Eddie a liberal and a humanist. He is ours, do you hear? Ours!"

Well, Eddie has admirable qualities that might make him a good president yet.

"Damn it, you have no right to be optimistic about Eddie. I demand that you show panic, horror, and trepidation about what he might do as president -- unleash right-wing assassins and vigilantes; allow the Americans to spread AIDS and birth control pills and PX goods through the bases, risk nuclear annihilation of the Filipino people. Come on, Larry, admit it, you are terrified!"

Oh come on, Small Dick, Marcos did all of that, and we survived him. The Americans also did all of that, and we still love them. So, what's new? What could Eddie Ramos and Kulas Platypus possibly do that Marcos and Bosworth have not already done?

"Damn it, Larry, you take all the fun out of our victory. One of these days, we will throw out the Americans and make you win. What do you think of that, asshole?"

Don't you dare, Small Dick. If we throw the Americans out, the Communists will be legalized and will probably shift their war into the parliamentary struggle. If so, as happened in Western Europe where Communists are allowed to participate in electoral contests, the Communists will never get more than six percent of the vote. In free elections, they always lose; in armed struggle, they often manage to win, but the nation always loses, as in Vietnam.

If we throw out the American bases and reduce the Communists to impotence, Small Dick, who else can we blame for all our failures?

If we cannot blame the Americans and the Communists for all our failures, then we will only have ourselves to depend on for salvation and survival. And that is hard work, Needle Dick, that's a hell of a lot of hard work!

And that will make you even more depressed, Small Dick.

December 23, 1988, Philippine Daily Inquirer

ooooo

CHAPTER 2. The Press Gridiron Night

Part 1. The Apotropaic rites

The time has come for the annual apotropaic rites. "Apotropaic" is a word unknown to writers and college dictionaries, having been invented by Larry Henares and the Webster's Unexpurgated Dictionary to irritate the rest of you out there. An apotropaic rite is one designed to ward off evil spirits, like sprinkling holy water on Friday the 13th, like lamb's blood smeared on the door on Passover, like driving a wooden stake into Dracula's heart, and like the ritual roasting of the President by the Press on Gridiron Night.

In the Press Gridiron Night, we gather as we do every year, to dispel the evil spirits of conflict and dissension among the ruler, the ruled and the rude. The ruler is the government. The ruled are the people. The rude of course are the rude members of the press who promote quarrels between the people and their government, and have the effrontery to act as referees in the fight.

In the Gridiron Night we dispel the evil spirits by being at peace with each other, that is by peacefully sleeping while listening to each other's corny jokes. On such a night we are witness as we always were in the past, to plays written by writers who cannot write, acted by actors who cannot act, comedians who think they are as funny as Secretary Flavier, and singers who sing like the promoters of Luciano Pavarotti

The organizers might present the young violinist Jay Cayuca who once in a concert by Baby Arenas, played a piece that Erap liked. When Erap was told that it was the Romeo and Juliet Overture composed by Tchaikovsky, he exclaimed, "Gee I didn't know Jaworsky could compose!" There are many other things the Gridiron organizers may do to make this night a Magnum Opus and an affair to remember.

They may arrange a real Roast of the President by actual critics playfully accusing him of faults they themselves are guilty of.

For instance, Max Soliven who is known as the greatest Filipino tourist of all time, may accuse Erap, as he did of Ramos, of going on too many state visits.

Julliet Yap Daza may decry Erap's tendency to "tell the people" yakkity-yak-yak instead of quietly doing his work and writing a book on sex everyone is too embarrassed to read.

Emil Jurado, who taught Erap Estrada the English language, may decry Erap's lack of oratorical eloquence.

Larry Sipin may wish Erap was more assertive and charismatic.

Baby Orosa may accuse Erap of sleeping through concerts and plays like she always does.

And finally Margie Go-Home may complain that Erap talks, talks, talks, instead of doing and doing and doing what seems to be always in her mind -- and not being able to stand up to her, Erap may just have to take her lying down.

Part 2. Sorry, wrong number

Upon the annual apotropaic rite of the Gridiron Night, the ritual roasting of the President of the Philippines, I in turn would like to make my wish-list for the press and the President for the coming year. I wish that in the coming year Erap will be less onion-skinned, less sensitive to press criticisms, less *pikon* than he sometimes seem to be. He should appreciate the vigilance of the press, and endure its hardboiled irreverence against the insolence of office. But let me advise the press in turn against cynicism, a lack of faith bordering on contempt by those who succumb to the trappings of power, even the power of the press. A newsman who surrenders to cynicism, loses his irreverence, his objectivity, and his humanity.

Lastly, I would like to share with them a joke about a Filipino official who called his house by long distance from Singapore and was answered by one of the servants. *"Hello,"* sabi niya, *"Gusto kong kausapin ang aking asawa!" Isang saglit po,* the boy answered, and after a while he returned to the phone and said, *"Sorry po, naka sara ang pinto, at hindi nila na rinig ang katok ko, kasi nag sisigawsigaw sila, yong asawa ninyo at kanyang kasamang lalaki."*

"Ganon ha? Hoy, alam mo kong saan naka tago ang susi ng pinto. Alam mo rin naka tago ang aking baril. Buksan mo ang pinto-an, at barilin mo ang dalawang yon."

After a while the boy reported, *"Tapos na po yon pinapagagawa ninyo." "Okay,"*sabi ng official, *"kunin mo yong dalawang bankay at itapon mo sa swimming pool."* Sagut naman ng boy, *"Swimming pool? Wala nanam tayo ng swimming pool, eh!"*

There was a moment's silence. Then the Filipino official asked, *"Teka, ano na itong teleponong tinawag ko? 817-2391?"* To which the boy answered, "Sorry wrong number!"

And the point of this story is that in many instances people in the press and some politicians like Joker Arroyo keep accusing Erap of doing things he did not really do. Erap's answer should , "Sorry, you have the wrong number."

Erap cannot speak for the press better than newsmen can. I always believed in voluntary self-policing by the members of the press themselves. Perhaps Joe Guevara is correct: better blow away the harsh realities of life in a gale of laughter, than distort the truth with malice. But I do wish that press heckling and sniping, however good-natured, be accompanied once in a while by a purposeful desire to build, not to destroy, our confidence in our President Erap, in ourselves, our nation and our people.

Mabuhay to you all! Mabuhay ang Filipinas!

Part 3. One year in Erap's lifetime

What is one year in the lifetime of a man? Measured in terms of the humdrum routines of everyday living one and a half years will pass like one and a half minutes, unnoticed, uncounted and unremembered. Measured in terms of new friendships found, of meaningful relations made, of important tasks performed, of great movements and noble purposes, one and a half years will pass like a whole lifetime, each moment counted and recounted in the vast storehouse of one's memory.

Such is the one year of Erap's association with you the people and his fellow workers in Malacañang since his inauguration as the new President of the Philippines. You are not only his countrymen, you are his friends and his family. As he approaches the end of his first year as our President, well may he greet all of us and thank us for the support we have given him, 67 percent approval rating, the highest ever earned by a president of our republic. Well may he thank us for sustaining him through all his mistakes and frustrations, and for contributing greatly to all his successes. Together we have helped lick the problem of crime and punishment, at long last giving teeth and meaning to the death penalty for heinous crimes. Together we have helped him prop up a sagging economy, stabilizing our currency rate while neighboring countries have reeled from the blow of the Asian currency crunch. Together we have helped him ward off the dissident threats to the Republic from the New People's Army who dared to kidnap our generals and officials, as well as from the MILF with its unremitting demand for political independence. Together we have helped him resolve the political problems in Congress, and have given the Filipino people hope and great expectations. And together we shall solve the many problems left: the traffic problem, the lack of housing, the lack of capital, and many others that might have daunted lesser men. And together we shall have led the nation to greater heights with the vision of Philippines 2000. *Kaya ba natin ito?* *Sagot kayo.* Louder, louder, let it echo to the far reaches of our nation to every Filipino.

[Nota Bene, 2002:   This was before we realized Erap was a thief]

Erap Estrada must appreciate the fact that his new team in Malacañang have rendered service beyond the call of duty in their respective offices. Most of them stay there till the wee hours of the morning dutifully finishing the work Erap needs the next day. Some of them come every day for five minutes, as Larry Henares did in the administration of Fidel Ramos, to get his assignment, because he is afraid that if he stays longer, he may receive a stab in the back by the few who indulge in intrigues. That's okay, he was paid only P1 a year. Lucky fellow, President Ramos did not give him a check for him to frame as a memento, because as Ramos explained, the check would cost P20 more. Instead, lucky Larry received P10 in cash, paper money on which Ramos scribbled: "Keep the change."

Part 4. Panay na Panay

All of us know that few of the Malacanang workers say they are working late in the Malacanang office even if they are not. Women do this to avoid having to go with people they do not like, "Comadre, sorry *hindi ako maka punta sa party mo, may trabaho ako sa oficina"* Some men do this to avoid their wives, "Darling, *huwag mo na ako hi-hintayin, at marami akong trabaho sa ofinina."*

But today they must relax, and have a party to celebrate Estrada's first year in office. They must thank the Lord for all his blessings, and ask him to take pity on the poor orphans who are fed so much by so many kind people during Christmas, that they suffer constantly from nausea, stomach ache and diarrhea, only to starve after the New Year.

Speaking of food, our former Secretary of Health, now a senator, sometimes acted as food taster to guarantee his President Fidel Ramos had the right food. Once in a classy restaurant, President Ramos ordered Peking Duck, but before he even began to eat, Secretary Flavier put his finger into the rear end of the duck, probed it, and said, "This duck is not genuine, it comes from Hong Kong. Waiter, bring us another one." The waiter brought another duck, and Flavier again put his finger inside the rear end of the duck, probed it and announced, "This duck comes from Taipei, not Peking. Bring us the real thing." The waiter brought a third duck. Flavier poked his finger in, and announced, "This duck is a real Peking duck. You may eat it, Mr. President." I am telling you this, because later that night, Flavier told a waitress, "How pretty you are. Where are you from?" And the waitress screamed, "Secretary Flavier, keep your finger to yourself!"

Speaking of places where one comes from, I was once a guest of a crowd of dumb people, not stupid but speechless, they were *pipi*. I asked where each came from. One hooked two fingers and I knew he came from Kawit, which means hook. Another knotted his fingers together like this, and I knew he came from Bohol, meaning knot. One made a cylinder with his left fingers and covered it with his right palm, and I knew he came from Tacloban, to cover. One scratched his belly, and I knew he was from Makati meaning itchy. Another made a motion that he came from Masbate. Dirty minds, I bet you thought he shook his right fist up and down like he was playing solitaire. No, you are wrong, he rubbed his two palms as if he was making "*bate*" a cup of Spanish chocolate. Then one made a cylinder with his left hand, and put his right finger into it, like this, and I know he came from Navotas (*Na butas*). And the last one made the same motion putting his finger in repeatedly! Aha, *panay na panay*, I said, you are from Panay!

Part 5. What he needed was Recognition

President Estrada should say to his fellow workers in Malacañang, "My friends, this is the time to express my gratitude and my appreciation for having your cooperation and encouragement during the first year of my administration. I want you to know that I appreciate the work you have done for me this year. Some of you take pleasure in doing good work in quantity, some enjoy doing quality work, some are motivated by recognition of their talents. Every one has his own motivation and need for gratification.

The story goes that there were three *baklas* discussing what gives them pleasure in doing their work. One said, "QUANTITY, just let me loose to work among all the soldiers in the Defense Department and I will appreciate the quantity." The second one said, "QUALITY, just let me work with that handsome hunk of a man like Fernando Poe Junior, and I will appreciate the quality." And the third one said, "What I like most is RECOGNITION, an appreciation of my talents by the highest official of the land." He was asked how he can manage that, and he explained, "Well, I'll go to President Erap Estrada and tell him that I will sell all my properties and contribute all my money to his Presidential Fund. Then I will tell him that I will abandon my friends and family to work for him alone, at all hours of the day and only for one peso a year. Then I will tell him that I will do anything he tells me to do, climb the highest mountain, swim the deepest ocean, or make the supreme sacrifice by jumping off a cliff. Then President Erap Estrada will look at me and say, *'Sipsip ka talaga, ano?'* That is RECOGNITION, said the bakla, my friends, that is real recognition!"

Well, I might as well tell you one more joke, a favorite of mine. A rich man had a daughter who got pregnant out of wedlock and he was determined to get rid of the unwanted child. So he went to the local hospital and offered the doctor a million pesos to get rid of the bastard: "Doctor," he instructed, "when the baby is born to my daughter, take it and give it to another mother giving birth at the same time. Tell my daughter her child was still-born, and tell the other woman that she just had twins, fraternal twins. For that I am giving you a million pesos." The doctor agreed.

When the day came, the daughter gave birth to a son, but there was no other woman giving birth at the same time. There was only this priest having his appendix removed. Well, to make the story short, the doctor said to himself, "what can I lose? I already was paid the million pesos. So *bahala na,* I will put this baby beside the priest and say, 'Congratulations, Father, you are a father!' "

To his surprise and delight, the priest took the baby boy home and cared for him like a real son. Twenty one years later, the priest called the young man to the sacristy and said, "Son, you are already 21 years old and you deserve to know the truth about yourself. People say I am your father. That is not true. I am not your father. I am your mother. The bishop is your father."

April 22 to 28, 1999, Philippine Post

ooooo

CHAPTER 3. My Message To The Graduating Class

Part 1. Goodbye To Your Teachers

In this day of days when you of the graduating class are about to leave the portals of your school out into the jungle world of earning a living, perhaps it would not be amiss to look back, and say goodbye to a time that will never be yours again. After today, the carefree time of your golden youth, will be gone forever.

Say goodbye to your teachers and professors. Someday, you will realize how much you owe them, these poor pathetic underpaid creatures whom you will leave behind. God bless the teachers. In the long list of God's creatures, aside from saints, fathers and mothers, there are none more deserving of heaven than our teachers. Confucius was a great teacher. Buddha was a great teacher. Jesus Christ was to us the greatest of all teachers. Priests and nuns are essentially teachers, and so are all the scientists, philosophers and geniuses of this world who pass on knowledge and wisdom, love and goodness, truth and beauty, from one generation to another throughout the ages.

I had great teachers in my day, teachers who filled my hours with the joy of learning... a history teacher, Father Horacio de la Costa, who on the very first day of class, said: "Let me tell you the story of nations, let me tell you of how civilization came into being, and the men and women who brought it about."

... an English teacher, Father James Reuter, who read Shakespeare's plays, playing all the roles, in voices ranging from falsetto to bass, jumping from place to place, fencing with imaginary enemies, embracing imaginary friends... and all of a sudden, Shakespeare came alive, his plays became instruments that searched men's hearts and souls, baring the splendor and the meanness of the human spirit, the soaring heights to which it can ascend and the miry depths to which it can sink.

... and my 4th grade teacher, Miss Teresa Benito who would say: "Children, in this class we shall learn arithmetic, the magic of numbers that will someday enable you to build a bridge, a towering skyscraper, and a space ship that will bring you to the stars."

God bless our teachers, celebrators of Life, harbingers of Civilization!

And also, members of the graduating class, do not

forget to thank your parents. Of course it is only too true that your parents brought you into this world without your knowledge and consent, and through an act of love done purely at their own pleasure.   Therefore the risk and consequences are theirs.

I need not remind you, young friends, that the dues have been paid many times over. Your parents have fully paid the price of being parents. Your mother paid early in the maternity ward and the many nights she had to wake up to feed you and to change your diapers. Your father paid his dues during the many overtime hours he worked himself to the bone to keep you safe and secure in home and hearth, to pay for your tuition, to give you an extra allowance, to finance your dates. And both your parents fully paid their dues the many times they sat worried to death when you came back home late at night, or when you had a serious illness, or when your behaviour and your grades were less than satisfactory. More tomorrow.

Part 2. Thank Your Parents

Think back right now, young friends, and see how your parents did influence your life and bring you to this point, to this very day when you are ready to go out on your own and to take responsibility for your own life.

My father was a great inventor, engineer, industrialist, and a wonderful father. Once, while I was brooding on some shameful deed, he put his arms around me and ever so gently said: "Please remember that nothing you can ever do, however evil, can ever make me love you less. If you ever get into trouble, never hesitate to tell me about it. And we shall see together how we can set it right, and prevent it from ever happening again."

A writer named Carlos Bulosan once wrote of the laughter of his father. I speak of the wonder of my father. Not only because to me and to many others, he was such a wonderful man, but also because he was a man so full of wonder --- full of the wonder of life itself, its challenges, its excitement, its grandeur and the innate goodness of its ultimate purpose. Full of the wonder of love which he lavished without counting the cost, on his family, his friends, his fellow industrialists, and above all, his native land which is also yours and mine.

God bless our parents, the fountainhead of our existence, the premordial source of love, of life itself, without whom none of us will be here today.

And now for the young graduates of this school, the honorees on this graduation day. What is in store for you? How can you cope with the future that awaits you? What can I tell you now that doesn't sound corny and trite and tiresome? What can I say that has not been said over and over again in thousands of graduation ceremonies for the last thousand years?

Firstly, you should realize that half of the education you had in college is making lifelong friends. In the last few years of your life, you have met in college those with whom you will do business in the future, those with whom you will spend your social life; people whom you have come to know, to depend on, and to trust; perhaps, even the special person whom you will marry and keep as a lifetime partner. In the last four years, you have met your best friends and your worst enemies, your wife, husband, partners and business associates, and those whom you know to be morons, cheats, scoundrels, and undependable friends. Keep in touch with your classmates and schoolmates long after you graduate from college, they are the keys to your future, as they are with Erap.

Secondly, you should realize that your education does not end upon graduation. In a way, it is only beginning, for the field that you will choose for your life's work, whether it be finance or accounting or marketing, is constantly evolving in new ways and new directions. To be educated is to learn how to learn by yourself, how to find what you need to learn on your own initiative to satisfy your own needs. That is the real meaning of Education. So, dear young friends, keep learning through books, through seminars, through interaction with your peers in professional organizations, be a student all the rest of your life.

Thirdly, you will find in the world outside that success will depend on certain qualities that you have developed in your school years. Often it is not brilliance of mind that will place you on top of the heap; you will find that the brightest in your class is often not the most successful. More tomorrow.

Part 3. The three levels of genius

The most successful in any graduating class are not the ones with the highest grades. You must realize that there are really three levels of genius, and the best of this is not the one that gets good grades.

First is the analytical genius; this is the pride of teachers and schools, the one with the highest grades and the uncanny ability to learn and teach knowledge. They make the best teachers and professors.

The second is the creative genius who is the despair of teachers and schools, because like Albert Einstein, Thomas Edison, Alexander Graham Bell, yes, even Leonardo da Vinci, they never seem to get good grades, but are responsible for innovations and inventions that change the world for the better.

Third, and probably the most important is the one considered street-smart, and not even classified as a genius, like President Erap Estrada. These are the ones never noticed by teachers and schools, those who organize dances, outings, elections, clubs and various extracurricular activities. And they are the most successful in life for they become kings, presidents and popes-- the not-so-bright who try harder to get ahead, the plodders, the ones who are dependable and trustworthy, who know how to get along with people and influence them to act towards a common goal, those with initiative, imagination and talent for organization and leadership. Above all, it is their Self Confidence that brings Success, a faith in oneself, a sense of destiny and pride that make possible the impossible.

My daughter Rosanna, when she was a little girl, wrote a poem that says just that. She wrote:

> *You are only as good as you think you are;*
> *Swiftness and Strength can only bring you so far.*
> *The race you run and the battle you plan ---*
> *You will only win if you think you can!*

What is true of individuals is true of nations too. The reason the Philippines is a nation of losers is that we have lost faith in ourselves, we have lost the sense of nationalism, the sense of common purpose and common destiny, the sense of belonging to each other, the national pride, the national conceit if you will, the creative conceit that makes possible the impossible.

Ask any Japanese which is the greatest country in the world, and he will answer: "Japan! We descended from the Sun God, and we beat the white men at their own game!" Ask the Chinese, and he will say: "China! We are the oldest surviving civilization, we were writing poetry while the white men were still living in caves and painting themselves blue." Ask the Indian, the Indonesian and the Thai --- and you will get the same answer.

The Americans are the most nationalistic people in the world. When an American says he is an American, he thumps his chest like Tarzan of the Apes. When a Filipino says he is a Filipino, he scratches his belly like Cheeta the Chimpanzee. For that is what a Filipino thinks of himself: Gunga Din to the White Father, Sabu the Elephant Boy to the Great White Hunter, Tonto *tarantado* to the Lone Ranger. Filipinos are real losers because in their minds they have already lost.

More tomorrow.

Part 4. The Past of Mankind leads to the Future

In this 100th anniversary of our nation's birth, it is well remind ourselves of the generation of magnificent young Filipinos a century ago, just barely 30 years of age, who challenged two of the greatest colonial powers – Spain and the United States – broke the shackles of Western colonialism, executed the first nationalist revolution in Asia, antedating the Chinese Double Ten by 13 years, and built a nation and the first democratic republic in all of Asia.   On the eve of the Third Millennium, it is the task your generation to recapture their spirit of nationalism, their sense of national purpose and national destiny.

What is ahead for Mankind and the world in the coming century and in the next millenium? As a sequel to Rizal's "The Philippines 100 Years Hence," let me extrapolate. Barring a nuclear war or a giant meteor hitting the earth that will end our existence, what is it in the past that portends what might happen in the future?

Man has certainly gone a long way from the time he emerged from the dusty plains of Africa some 100 million years ago, walking upright and populating the entire planet earth. He wandered over the entire world by running away from his shit, which polluted the ground he lived in and caused plagues and diseases. His brain began to expand when he learned to eat the 21 varieties of mushrooms that grow out of the shit of animals, full of hallucinatory drugs that blew his mind into dreams of past, future and the abstract world.

He earned his living by hunting animals and plucking fruits out of the trees. If he continued earning his living that way, only 25 million of his kind can exist on limited resources of this planet. Fortunately for him, in the valleys of the Nile, the Tigris and the Euphrates rivers, people learned to domesticate animals and plant crops for food, and agriculture was born. Today agriculture supports most of mankind, which has grown to 5 and a half billion in population, most of them living a marginal existence because the resources of the earth are already stretched to the limit. Fortunately again in England of the 16th century the Industrial Revolution was born, and machines and factories took over from muscles and sweat, and production and consumption of goods increased geometrically. But unfortunately this resulted in the ravage and rape of Mother Earth, its air and waters polluted, its mountains disemboweled for minerals, the fertility of its lands exhausted and leached by chemicals. Suddenly the Malthusian prediction that the population explosion will soon outrun the resources of the earth has become a great probability, causing as he predicted, wars, plagues and pestilence to reduce man's population. In the face of this, in the face of the population of the earth doubling every thirty years, what is the prognosis for the future of Man and his planet??

Part 5. The Last Frontier is the Sea

Either Man will go forth and populate other planets, or he goes back to where he came from – the sea, from which his progenitors evolved.   For the sea is the last frontier, comprising three fourths of the area of the planet Earth. On land we progressed from hunter to farmer to industrial worker. In the sea, we are still hunters. There in the sea are unlimited resources awaiting exploitation. The water cycle by which water rises from the sea as vapor, then falls on land as rain, washes the resources of the land and spews them toward the sea, and leaves them there, accumulating under our oceans a wealth of minerals unimagined and unimaginable. There in the sea the vast energy of sunlight generates plankton that feeds the fishes that feed other fishes up to the top of the food chain, the great fishes and Man himself.

Someday we will all go back to the sea. There we will build great undersea mines to scoop minerals from the bottom of the sea, there to drill wells even as we do now for oil and gas. There with sound waves, we can set up undersea fences within which we will domesticate fishes just as we do the cows and goats and lambs on land. And if there is no longer any space on land, we can even build great undersea cities much easier than we can build one on the moon and the planets.

The sea is our last frontier and it is only exploitable in that part of the ocean called the Continental Shelf, the shallow part where the beaches slope gradually until they reach a sudden drop called the Ocean Trench and the Ocean Deep. There are only a few Continental Shelves in the world. In Northern Europe there is only one, the North Sea where oil is being drilled, too small and too cold to support a continent. Then there is the Mediterranean Sea Shelf, warm and large enough to support South Europe and North Africa. In the United States and the Americas there is only the Mexican and Texas Gulf, too small to support two continents.

The greatest Continental Shelf in the world is in the Pacific, bounded by the Mindanao Trench to the East, the Spratleys to the West, Taiwan to the North, and Borneo to the South. And striding over it like a Magnificent Colossus is our own country the Philippines. The Philippines itself is an undersea valley where the islands are the tips of undersea mountains. By the UN Law of the Sea we are accorded an economic development zone of 200 miles beyond our land boundaries. Thus in the future the world will beat a path to the Philippines to buy the resources with which to feed itself in the next hundred years, in the next thousand years. And we will not be found wanting, for we and the world are on the verge of the Information Age.

During the Industrial Revolution, advanced nations become richer and the poor nations become poorer, because poor nations depend on their natural resources which are depletable, while advanced nations depend on <u>skills and knowledge</u>, which are not only non-depletable but also transferable. The more you use your skills, the more skilled you become; the more you use your knowledge, the more knowledgeable you are. And such skills and knowledge are transferable; if I teach you how to make a camera, I will be giving you something I myself do not lose- the ability to make a camera. But poor nations compelled to contribute their resources like iron ore, are using up something they forever lose. Thus advanced nations like Japan can import from us iron ore at $25 per ton and make machinery valued at $5,000 out of it, contributing nothing to the value but their skills and knowledge, resources that are ever augmented. Thus Japan gets richer while we stand barefooted on the richest soil on earth.

In the Information Age, with the advent of computers and communications satellites, managerial techniques and mass educational facilities, poor nations can learn those skills and knowledge that make advanced nations great. If we find out how to make our own machinery, why should we export our iron ore to Japan? Thus in the Information Age when every nation and people on earth accumulate the skills and knowledge needed to survive, then the economic power will gravitate back from advanced nations to the nations with the most exploitable resources.

Part 6. The Philippines 100 Years Hence

The Philippines is destined to be the greatest nations on earth. Don't laugh, my friends. Nations are born, they grow old and eventually die. So it was with Egypt, Greece, Rome, England, and so it will be with Mother America. Civilization is passed from mother to son, colonizer to colonized, from one nation to another since the dawn of time, from Egypt the builder of pyramids, across the Aegean Sea to the Glory that was Greece, across the Mediterranean Sea to the Grandeur that was Rome, across the European continent to the Atlantic seaboard, where civilization was passed on to two great colonial powers, Spain and England. Both crossed the Atlantic in separate paths to the New World; Spain to South and Central America; and England to North America where it passed the torch to the great United States. Both

Spain and the United States crossed the Pacific and the paths of civilization co-joined in the Philippines, their only Asian colony. Greatness beckons to the worst of us. Egyptians were dirt farmers, Greeks were goat-herders, Romans were Etruscan pot makers, the English were barbarians who lived in caves and painted themselves blue, the Americans were convicts, misfits and the wretched of Europe, and we Filipinos are lazy bums.

Do you doubt now, my friends, that destiny will pass the torch of civilization in the next century and millenium into our hands?? To the Filipinos, now scattered all over the world in our New Diaspora, the Wandering Jews of the future, and the First Citizens of a Brave New World??

Once upon a time after their Babylonian Captivity, the Jews were forcibly driven from their homeland in Palestine, and forcibly scattered all over a hostile world. In what was called their Diaspora, these Wandering Jews found themselves unwelcome everywhere, forced to live in segregated ghettoes, persecuted and massacred in pogroms, and programmed for extinction in Hitler's Final Solution. But a few of them managed to survive their 2,000 year ordeal, and those who survived, according to Charles Darwin's evolutionary principle of Natural Selection, were the wisest, shrewdest, strongest, hardiest and most adaptable of the race. Theories of racial superiority promulgated by the Teutonic races of the world, the Germans, Dutch, English and the Americans, tend to be out of fashion nowadays. But if there is such a superior race, it would certainly be the Jews who have won more than their rightful share of Nobel prizes, of wealth and power, of significant contributions to the arts and sciences. Of the 26 geniuses with an IQ of over 170 in New York City, all are Jewish.

Like the Jews, we Filipinos are being forced by economic need to go all over the world, as workers, engineers, doctors, nurses, musicians, domestics and nannies – for the most part resented and outlawed, murdered and persecuted. But somehow like the Jews, we survive and prosper, because we are adaptable, skilled, literate, and proficient in English, the lingua franca of the world. As such we are the last of the Noble Savages and the First Citizens of the World, as Julian Huxley wrote in his novel, The Brave New

World.

Thus we predict that in the next millenium we will see our own, our native land, the Philippines, astride the greatest Continental Shelf on earth, with most of the resources of the sea under its control, become a truly Great Power.

Part 7. I am Youth. Heed me, the future is mine

My dear friends, you will soon enter college and a labor market at the time of our Great Economic Crisis, brought about mostly by policies forced upon our technocrats by the IMF, the World Bank and the Americans. It is unfortunate that under the Cory Administration, the disastrous policies of the IMF and Marcos continued to drive our economy to perdition. Our technocrats like Joey Cuisia and Jesus Estanislao do not care; they only look forward like Gerardo Sicat to be rewarded with a minor position in the World Bank, there to be highly paid in tax free non devaluable dollars.

And it is up to you of this generation to do what the generation of the 1950s did when they were faced with same kind of economic crisis. They fought back under the aegis of Economic Nationalism to build an industrial economy that was the envy of Asia, especially of Taiwan and Korea. Taiwan was then a primitive backwater refuge of the defeated Kuomintang armies, and Korea was going through the madness of a civil war. Today these two countries whose combined population is less than that of the Philippines, are exporting ships, computers and whole factories, while the Philippines was sold out to the Americans and the IMF, forced now to dismantle its industries and go back to a plantation type of colonial economy based on yellow corn, buntal hats, mail order brides and ipil ipil.

It is the task of your generation to reverse this act of treason, to decolonize our economy and set it once more toward industrialization, social justice and economic progress. In the words of W.H. Auden the poet, "Clear from the head the masses of impressive rubbish,/ Rally the lost and trembling forces of the will,/ Gather them up and let them loose upon the earth/ Until they construct at last a human justice."

In the last two presidential elections, the only ones with courage to advocate Economic Nationalism are Jovito Salonga and Joseph Estrada. The rest play it safe by saying

Amen to the IMF.

My young friends, get up from your crawling belly, plant your two feet on this plot of solid earth, fold your arms across you breast and say, as a young man named Raul Manglapus once said when our nation was yet unborn and when he had not yet capitulated to the Americans on the bases:

"I am Youth. I am he who dreams but who shall make your dreams come true. I am he who shall take the green of your pastures, the gold of your hills, the might of your rivers -- fashion them with my hands, my heart, my mind and transform them into life and power. I am he who shall take this nation which you will someday bequeath to me, breathe into it the warmth of my ideals, build it firm and strong and higher up to the stars till the universe shall know of its strength. I am he who shall think, work, act --- until the Filipino Tao, ill starred and striped no longer in the prison garb of self doubt and colonial double allegiance, shall stand head high in pride and dignity on every field and valley of this land. I am a laborer, I am a builder, I am a dreamer. I am Youth! Heed me, for the future is mine!"

March 27, 1999, University of Northwestern Philippines, Iriga, Camarines Sur

April 16 to 21, 1999, ISYU.

ooooo

CHAPTER 4. Sexual Harassment and the Mating Game

Part 1. "It's not my fault, Father, he forced me"

Sex and violence on children are taboo in these days of child abuse and pedophilia. But how about the children themselves as aggressors? Two boys aged ten were found to have murdered a two year old toddler cruelly and needlessly.

But here is strange one. According to Newsweek, 6-year old Johnathan Prevette was charged with sexual harassment for kissing a little girl on the cheek. This is probably a hoax or a misunderstanding. Six year old boys do not like girls. They are all male chauvinist pigs, girl bashers, teasers, taunters, vandals, bullies, and the cutest kids in the world. Mary Ann Clausen recalls that as a little girl in 1937, she was seated behind the little boy Curtis. One day she tapped him on the shoulder and showed him a piece of paper on which was written "I love you." Whereupon Chris reacted and punched her. She reported this to the teacher who advised her to hit him back. And she did, she took him to the porch and belted him a haymaker.

If this happened in 1996, Mary Ann and Curtis would have been involved in law suits by their parents, and sent to psychiatrists for counseling, and the teacher would have been investigated and temporarily relieved of her duties for encouraging violence. The contemporary rules, tested in court cases, are "No Touch," and no female advances on innocent males.

It is even more ridiculous when applied to the mating game. Everybody knows the basic strategy of the husband-hunting female: start by resisting the man's advance, then end up by blocking his retreat. No girl consents to be kissed on the first date, otherwise she may be considered "cheap."

In a Catholic guilt-ridden country like the Philippines, girls entice their boyfriends to kiss and make love to them while feigning resistance, for a religious reason. They do not have to confess it to the priest as a sin, "It is not my fault, Father, he forced me." Thus the girls remain guiltless of a sin they thoroughly enjoy committing.

Thus the mating game is played. Stealing kisses is almost always necessary as a first step in courting. And tempting the boy is part of the arsenal of the deadly female, drooping eyes with a sigh, wearing perfume and bending over close enough for a quick kiss. And she does this whether she wants to be kissed or not, "I may not want to be kissed, but I certainly want him to try. It is good for my ego. And I reserve the right to express my pleasure or displeasure, after the fact. I have him at a psychological disadvantage."

My experience in my youth is that it is worth the risk, If she did not want to be kissed, or is offended by bad breath or body odor, the worst she would do is to slap me. Or tell her boyfriend to take it out of my hide. A fist fight on a one to one basis at most, no knives, no guns, no baseball bats.

Today the rules are different. If she resists, even if she

is only pretending to do so, it is legally considered sexual harassment. And if she decides to give the boy trouble, for any reason whatsoever, then there is hell to pay, in disciplinary measures by the office or school, in the newspapers, in the courts.

Part 2.   In cases of sexual abuse, the female has the advantage

Of course, it is the human right of every person to be liberated from sexual harassment or abuse. We have seen bosses who take advantage of their employees.

While his secretary was typing his letter, the boss reached down from behind her into her dress and grabbed both her boobs. Weakly she protested, "Please, don't." He laughed and said, "Give me ten reasons." She said, "Somebody might see us." That's one reason, he challenged, nine more. And she had to recite all the ten reasons she could think of (it's a sin, your wife will get mad, It's a scandal, I'll scream) before he actually let go. This really and actually happened, it sounded funny at the time, but it was not, it was sexual harassment in the working place.

We have seen sexual abuse of young maids by drivers, houseboys, gardeners -- for which they pay dearly by being forced into matrimony and a lifetime of embattled togetherness. Not to mention abuse by the man of the house or his sons. And the poor abused girls have no recourse but to quit their jobs and go back to the provinces to bear the fruits of their misfortune.

Ah, but nowadays the girls are back with a vengeance. Encouraged by the advances in contraception and even by abortion, and by society's permissiveness and propensity for court litigation, they now enjoy a leveled playing field. Not really, they enjoy a distinct advantage.

When a woman complains of being sexually abused, it is legally presumed that she would not suffer the shame of public exposure unless her charges are true and she has no other recourse in seeking justice. She owns her body, and if she is kissed or made love to while offering resistance, feigned or not, real or not, the law presumes she and only she is in possession of the truth of her feelings. If she says her resistance is real, her word is taken at its face value, no matter if the male feels that he has been deliberately tempted, challenged, and encouraged according to the accepted practices of the past. The Filipino word is "*pikot.*"

Because of the risk of being publicly pilloried as a sex maniac, the male must protect himself. There should be printed forms, contracts that should be signed before any dates or preliminary acts of courtship, defining the limits of behavior acceptable to both without invading the realm of sexual abuse or harassment. Contract No. 1, for instance, should provide that kissing or snuggling are allowable but the male should not let his hands wander below the neckline. Contract No. 2 may discourage any male venture below the waistline of the woman. Contract No. 3, by mutual consent should allow everything else, all systems go.

In this way, there is clear understanding and a distinctly charted path, but no more explorations and adventures into the unknown, no more excitement and surprises that add to the enjoyment. The battle of the sexes has deteriorated into choreographed dance.

Pity.

Part 3. The future of sex is masturbation?

The advantage of the female is furthered by differences in the anatomy of sex. In the famous case of the People versus the heavyweight champion Michael Tyson, the court ruled that it matters not if the girl consents to accompany Tyson to his hotel room, it matters not if both of them are already naked and ready for the sex act. If at the point when Tyson is all fired up to enter the woman's body, the girl yells stop, then he should stop. If he continues what comes naturally, he is guilty of rape, and may be sent to prison for six years.

By God, a woman can stop her sex drive any time she wants, but the man? My God, any full blooded man knows, really knows, that at some point in the mating game, at some point of no return, his mind loses control of his body, and that thing between his legs achieves a life and a will of its own, independent of his reason and desire. At that point six wild horses and all the king's men cannot dissuade it or divert it from its destined path. In all creation -- man, animal or vegetable -- the instinct for survival is suspended in the face of the urgency of the preservation of the species. Wars and duels are fought, and men and nations die, for the privilege of having an orgasm. Poor Mike Tyson should have considered the alternative of sex solitaire or masturbation.

A significant factor has entered the sex equation: the horror of AIDS, contagious and incurable, passed on through body contact and body fluids like semen, saliva and blood. No one is safe. When a person makes love to another, man and woman, gays and dykes, he or she is literally making love to all the persons the partner had relations with. The plague is passed on also by other means, blood transfusion, the birth process, baby's milk, excretion, mutual sex stimulation -- all in all, at such a geometric rate that every person is a potential carrier of the disease. This fear alone, even with the use of condoms, is enough to dampen the spontaneity and joy of human love, heterosexual or homosexual. Human contact of any sort is potentially a great danger. Perhaps the future of sex is masturbation.

Consider this. Scientists are presenting us the alternative of test tube babies. Actually even now, we can fertilize human eggs *in vitro* (in test tubes) without sex. We can ensure that fetuses are without disease and genetic defects. We can bring the fetuses to term and birth from the wombs of surrogate mothers.

Consider this. Today we have sex aids such as dildos, vibrators, lifelike inflatable mechanized sex partners that make self administered sex possible, even enjoyable. Experts say the solitaire sex allows one to proceed at his own pace without having to synchronize with another person, at best a chancy proposition. It certainly is less dangerous than cavorting with the neighbor's wife.

Not so, says Senator Kit Tatad my favorite Opus Dei member. He asserts that fornication, adultery and polygamy may be allowed, even forgiven, for God's chosen such as King David, conqueror of Goliath. But masturbation or onanism? It is so abhorrent to Jehovah that the only known character in the Bible who spilt his seed on the ground, Onan himself, was struck dead by the Lord, no ifs, no buts, without warning, *walang awa, walang kiyaokiyao.*

Me, I prefer the old fashioned mating game before Sex Liberation.   *October 21 to 23, 1996, ISYU* oooooo

CHAPTER 5. Holy Wars

Part 1. Bigotry versus religious tolerance

"In the beginning was Isis, oldest of the old; she was the goddess from whom all becoming arose." Thus started the Cult of Isis 5,000 years before Christ was born. For 5,000 years, all religions were founded on the Female Principle -- Isis in Egypt, Gaea in Greece, Terra in Rome, Shakti in the Hindu world – all based on the concept of Mother-Creator --- a concept that still crops up when we speak of Mother Earth, Motherland, Mother Nature, Mother Church. In the insect world, we see the Queen Bee and Queen Ant from whom all existence emanates. And it is Mama from whose body we derive life, sustenance and inspiration, whose nearness keeps us warm and glowing through all the adversities of life.

Fathers symbolize justice and discipline; but it is from our mothers that we seek tolerance, understanding, mercy, forgiveness. The Mother-Creator was a tolerant God, devoid of bigotry and aversion to sex, democratic in her acceptance of all other gods into her pantheon. There were more than 2,000 gods each in the Egyptian, Greek, Roman and Hindu temples. And for 5,000 years, there were no religious persecutions or holy wars. Civilizations flowered – Ancient Egypt, the Glory that was Greece, the Grandeur that was Rome, and the gentle philosophy of Buddhism and Hinduism of ancient India and China.

The Jews introduced the Male Principle, Jehovah the Father-Creator who was a jealous and avenging God, intolerant of other Gods, guilty of favoritism in his choice of his chosen people, ordering Abraham to kill his son, assassinating Onan for masturbating, devastating the earth with a Great Flood, and forcing David to cut 200 foreskins from penises of the poor Philistines. The elimination of the Mother Principle by Judaism and its derivatives, Christianity and Islam, was profoundly unsettling on human civilization, and led straight to the Dark Ages, the Crusades, the witch-hunts of Salem and the Holy Inquisition, the Jihads, and the religious wars of Ireland, Bosnia, India and the Middle East. For most of its history, Christianity has had a worse record than Islam, spilling more blood for religion's sake than the Muslim world did. But Europe's religious wars as well as the excesses of religious zeal in America, taught most Christians the futility of fighting to the death for something beyond human understanding and reason. And so was enshrined in the democratic constitution the principle of religious freedom and tolerance, and the separation of church and state. The Muslims never shared the same experience, and today are still fighting the same religious wars that will someday lead them to freedom and tolerance.

Despite President Bush's assurances to the contrary, the war on terrorism is a religious war. But it is not Christianity and Judaism versus Islam. It is primarily as it was centuries ago, a war between religious freedom and religious intolerance, between constitutionalism and fundamentalism, between the Mother Principle and the Father Principle. It is the same war libertarians are waging against the more virulent strains of Christian fundamentalism – Jerry Fallwell of the Bible Belt who fulminates against "the pagans, and the abortionists, and the feminists, and the gays and lesbians, the Civil Liberties Union -- all of them who have tried to secularize America" whom he blames for the terrorist attackon the Twin Towers on September 11, 2001. And the Opus Dei who burn books, practice self-mortification and believe there is no salvation outside of the Opus Dei and the Catholic Church.

It is the same war that Muslim fundamentalists waged and won against the Shah of Iran and in Afghanistan, and is still fighting against civil authority in every Muslim country in the world, against Israel and against the western world.

Part 2. The World of Absolute Truth from an essay by Andrew Sullivan

We may disagree with the fundamentalism of the Taliban and the likes of Jerry Fallwell and Pat Robertson and the Opus Dei, but we must admit it has attracted millions of adherents for centuries, and for a good reason. It provides comfort and certainty, and a sense of meaning and direction in the disorienting confusion and doubts of the modern world. Literal interpretations of the Bible and Koran written millenniums ago, the subjugation of reason and judgment and even conscience to the dictates of dogma, have an exhilarating effect on the flow of adrenalin, and have for centuries led men to perform extraordinary acts of both good and evil.

There is absolute logic to this. If you believe in life after death and the endless tortures of hell for those who disobey God's law, then you must conform to each diktat and encourage if not coerce others to do the same. It is not crazy to act this way if you believe these things strongly enough. In some ways, it's crazier to believe these things and not act this way.

In a world of absolute truth, in matters graver than life and death, there is no room for dissent and no room for theological doubt. Hence the reliance on literal interpretations of texts -- because interpretation can lead to error, and error can lead to damnation. Hence also the Catholic insistence on absolute church authority and papal infallibility. Without infallibility, there can be no guarantee of truth. Without such a guarantee, confusion can lead to hell.

Dostoyevsky's Grand Inquisitor makes the case perhaps as well as anyone. In the story told by Ivan Karamazov in the book "'The Brothers Karamazov," Jesus returns to earth during the Spanish Inquisition. On a day when hundreds have been burned at the stake for heresy, Jesus performs miracles. Alarmed, the Inquisitor arrests Jesus and imprisons him with the intent of burning him at the stake as well. What follows is a conversation between the Inquisitor and Jesus. Except it isn't a conversation because Jesus says nothing. It is really a dialogue between two modes of religion, an exploration of the tension between the Absolute Truth of religion and men's inability to live up to it, or even fully believe in it.

According to the Inquisitor, Jesus' crime was revealing that salvation was possible but still allowing humans the freedom to refuse it. And this, to the Inquisitor, was a form of cruelty. When the truth involves the most important things imaginable -- the meaning of life, the fate of one's eternal soul, the difference between good and evil -- it is not enough to premise it on the capacity of human choice. That is too great a burden. Choice leads to unbelief or distraction or negligence or despair.

What human beings really need is the certainty of truth,

and they need to see it reflected in everything around them -- in the cultures in which they live, enveloping them in a seamless fabric of faith that helps them resist the terror of choice and the abyss of unbelief. This need is what the Inquisitor calls the "fundamental secret of human nature" – the need to find "something that all would believe in and worship; what is essential is that all may be together in it. This craving for community of worship is the chief misery of every man individually and of all humanity since the beginning of time."

This is the voice of fundamentalism – of Absolute encompassing Truth that must be believed by all men or die as an unbeliever.

Part 3. The Voice of Fundamentalism, from an essay by Andrew Sullivan

This is the voice of fundamentalism. Faith cannot exist alone in a single person. Indeed, faith needs others for it to survive -- and the more complete the culture of faith, the wider it is, and the more total its infiltration of the world, the better.

It is hard for us to wrap our minds around this today, but it is quite clear from the accounts of the Inquisition and, indeed, of the religious wars that continued to rage in Europe for nearly three centuries, that many of the fanatics who burned human beings at the stake were acting out of what they genuinely thought were the best interests of the victims.

With the power of the state, they used fire, as opposed to simple execution, because it was thought to be spiritually cleansing. A few minutes of hideous torture on earth were deemed a small price to pay for helping such souls avoid eternal torture in the afterlife. Moreover, the example of such government-sponsored executions helped create a culture in which certain truths were reinforced and in which it was easier for more weak people to find faith.

The burden of this duty to uphold the faith lay on the men required to torture, persecute and murder the unfaithful. And many of them believed, as no doubt some Islamic fundamentalists believe, that they were acting out of mercy and godliness.

This is the authentic voice of the Taliban. It also finds itself replicated in secular form. Not only in the McCarthyism of the 1950s in the United States that destroyed the lives of those who disagreed with the exigencies of the Cold War, but also in other tyrannies.

What, after all, were the totalitarian societies of Nazi Germany or Soviet Russia if not an exact replica of this kind of fusion of politics and ultimate meaning? Under Lenin's and Stalin's rules, the imminence of salvation through revolutionary consciousness was in perpetual danger of being undermined by those too weak to have faith -- the bourgeois or the kulaks or the intellectuals. So they had to be liquidated or purged.

Similarly, it is easy for us to dismiss the Nazis as evil, as they surely were. It is harder for us to understand that in some twisted fashion, they truly believed that they were creating a new dawn for humanity, a place where all the doubts that freedom brings could be dispelled in a rapture of racial purity and destiny. Hence the destruction of all dissidents and the Jews -- carried out by fire as the Inquisitors had before, an act of purification different merely in its scale, efficiency and Godlessness.

Perhaps the most important thing for us to realize today is that the defeat of each of these fundamentalisms required a long and arduous effort. The conflict with Islamic fundamentalism is likely to take as long. For unlike Europe's religious wars, which taught Christians the futility of fighting to the death over something beyond human understanding and so immune to any definitive resolution, there has been no such educative conflict in the Muslim world.

Only Iran and Afghanistan have experienced the full horror of revolutionary fundamentalism, and only Iran has so far seen reason to moderate to some extent. From everything we see, the lessons Europe learned in its bloody history have yet to be absorbed within the Muslim world. There, as in 16th-century Europe, the promise of purity and salvation seems far more enticing than the mundane allure of mere peace.

That means that we are not at the end of this conflict but in its very early stages. For the world, the worst is still to come.

Dec. 12 to 14, 2001, on DWBR-FM

ooooo

CHAPTER 6. Carlota, they also suck who sit and wait

THEY suck. All those lazy bums in the government who sit on their fannies and do nothing, while the world of business grinds down to a halt.

Frankly I do not see why government officials are so insufferably arrogant when their roles in society are that of barnacles, leeches and bloodsuckers. They do not produce anything worthwhile -- not even a nail or a pin. They push papers around like scavengers and garbage collectors, and achieve nothing that in any way advances the progress of the human race.

They are dung.

Take these characters Fawziya M. Bagis and Abraham D. Ututalum, cashier and manager of the Makati branch of Philippine Amanah Bank who issued a bank manager's check of P14.74 million that bounced like one of Rey Reyes' rubber balls.

The check was issued in favor of Celebrity Travel and Tours, in payment for the airline tickets of Muslim Pilgrims to Mecca, and was dishonored by the bank upon presentation for payment, because of an ``honest mistake.''

A bank manager's check is no ordinary check, it is supposed to be as good as liquid cash, and to dishonor it is like declaring one genuine P500 bill not negotiable.

The issuers may have good reasons for canceling it, and may not be criminally liable for graft and corruption -- but the Central Bank must act on the complaint because it undermines the integrity of the entire banking system.

On December 29, 1988, Jaime A. Brillantes, CB Assistant Director, acknowledged the receipt of a letter complaint addressed to his boss Deputy Governor Carlota P. Valenzuela of the Central Bank. "Rest assured," Brillantes answered Fouzi A. Bondagjy, president of Celebrity Tours, "that we will look into this matter and will inform you of the result of our investigation as soon as possible."

That was more than NINE MONTHS AGO, and no

results are forthcoming from Brillantes and Valenzuela. Like every other lazy unfeeling useless official of our republic, they just sit and wait for someone to light a fire under their asses.

They suck -- all these indolent bums and inert sloths who are paid with our taxpayer's money and do nothing but sit and wait for their paychecks. They suck.

Of all these bloodsuckers the worst are those in the Customs. Louella S. Garcia of Pamplona writes in anguish about a package that was sent to her via Ace Shipping Co. by her husband last March 25. That's more than SIX MONTHS ago, and it is still rotting in the piers, awaiting Mison's signature.

She writes in Ilonggo: *"Permi gid ako nagatawag sa office sang Ace Shipping kag ang permi nila nga sagut na hindi pa napermahan ni Com. Mison."*

Even worse is the experience of Ms. Mila M. Guinto of Bonuan Catacdang, Dagupan, a registered nurse married to Lito, an engineer. Both of them worked in Saudi Arabia, and shipped their personal effects consisting of seven boxes containing a Betamax, stereo, and clothings worth P200,000.

The packages arrived in the Philippines on August 4, 1987 -- that is more than TWO YEARS ago. Some customs personnel now say that the cargo was used by the shipper to pay his taxes because the shipping firm went bankrupt. That is a lot of dung. These assholes in the Customs are fooling her, and are not doing the job for which they are being paid.

These shenanigans are more the rule than the exception. More than the Communists or the Separatists or the Makati Business Club or the Council of Trent, these lazy bums in our government, these barnacles, leeches and bloodsuckers, are our worst enemies.

Every time they touch our life, they contaminate it, they blight it like a plague. They are anathema, they are a curse upon the earth.

Make a shit list of all these dungheaps and send it somehow to the NPA Sparrow Units, with the suggestion that these rascals be castrated, disemboweled, doused with gasoline, set on fire, and buried alive, so we all can dance over their graves with spiked boots.

Forgive the irate outburst, dear reader. We Filipinos are so inured to these excreta that we have become numb with ennui, we have lost our capacity for righteous anger.

It is bad enough that the IMF has reverted our economy back to colonial dependence and subsistence agriculture. It is bad enough that our Army has degenerated into avenging angels of American Imperialism, massacring our nationalists, priests and humanists to advance the purposes of the CIA. It is bad enough to have a Congress of sniveling idiots, crooks and traitors.

By God, do we have to suffer too the yoke of a government that does not do its job? Do we have to acquiesce to a bureaucracy of lazy bums, barnacles, leeches, bloodsuckers and parasites?

How can we get these monkeys off our backs?

October 11, 1889

Ooooo

CHAPTER 7. Arthur Young is as American as Pancit Canton

Anderson means "the son of Andrew"; Richardson, the son of Richard; Wilson or Williamson, the son of William; Johnson, Jackson, Benson, Thompson have obvious derivations; Abenson comes from "Automatic appliances, Benito Lim & Sons" -- all these are patronyms, names derived from ancestors' names.

But not Tuason, Lacson, or originally Chinese names with a suffix -son. These are derived from the Chinese word "son" which means "wind" or "current" and is generally associated with Chinese descendants of families that came with the Limahong expedition, crossing the China Sea, driven by a favorable wind and current, and landing in the Lingayen Gulf.

These families are designated numerically. The prefix I- indicates the numeral One; Di-, the numeral Two; San- is Three; Si- is Four; Go- is Five. Therefore Ison or Hizon (of Negros and Pampanga) is the first family; Dizon (of Pampanga) is the second; Samson (Technical Institute) is third; Sison or Singson (presently Press Secretary and CB Governor, of Lingayen) is fourth; Gozon (Macapagal's

Secretary of Agriculture) is fifth. By the same token, Lacson (of Negros) is sixth; Chitson, or Quizon is seventh; Pecson (the very first lady Senator Imay Pecson from Pangasinan) is eighth; Kawson is ninth.

In addition, Tuason (of Quezon City) means leader, or elder, or *cuya*. Bengzon means clear as water, a good name for Pangasinan's legal luminarties -- Supreme Court Justice Jose Bengson, his sons lawyer Peps and ex-Secretary of Health Alran. Biason means a small fish, a funny name for a 6-foot general, now a senator. Suzon means defeated. Jocson {founder of MLQ University) means lucky. Sioson means younger, junior, bonso. Puzon (of Lingayen) means immensely wealthy. Tecson means slender as a bamboo, which amply describes our small-waisted banker Wilfredo.

Quimson (of Alaminos, Pangasinan) means golden. Tingson means lamp, lantern, something shining. Tiongson means noble, fair, middle. Bauson means dumpling; Banzon (maiden name of Magsaysay's widow) means 10,000. Quezon means family, to add, to increase, which does not describe the Manuel Quezon family, reduced to very few in number. The word typhoon is derived from Tai Son, meaning Big Wind. Just as Tai pan (big businessman) means a big achiever.

There are many Filipino words derived from the Chinese. Inchik, for instance, means Uncle, one held in admiration, a sign of respect. Hikao, earring means ear hook. Buaya, Ate (Atsi, elder sister), Ditsi (second sister), Satsi (third) sister. Cuya (A-hya),

Tao means bean. So Tao-yo or toyo means bean sauce. Tao-ho means bean cake. Tao-gue means bean sprouts. Go means cow, To means stomach; Go-to means the stomach of the cow.

And so on and so on.

Nowadays, the young Chinese are no longer given Filipino first names; in recognition of our colonial mentality, they are now given Anglo-Saxon names like Washington, Wellington and William. Such names as Robin Tong and John Wayne Go became common. Yang became Young, as in Baldwin Young and Arthur Young, friends of mine who are about as American as pancit canton. This gives rise to many interesting combinations:

There other interesting names of actual persons; Edgar Allan Pe, Ivan Ho, Robin Ho, Tiger Wu, Magic Tiongson (Johnson), Michael Joe Tan (Jordan).

Inseparable friends are Kenneth Sy and Andy Lim who are known to their Filipino associates as Cannot See and Ang Dilim! There are Bob Uy (Baboy), Ivan Ho and Robin Hoo. Sisters Solita Yu and Sophia Yu are collectively referred to as "You So-and-So."

The Sy family in turn has such names as Karen Sy (Currency) who is destined to be in the banking business; Constance Sy (constancy) who will be a housewife; Nick Roman Sy (necromancy) who will be in funeraria and faith-healing business. William Yu Sy is called "Will You See?"

The Go family has Stephen Go (Step and Go) and Gawain Go (nicknamed by friends, Ga-Go). The Ngo girl who married a Ngo boy is named Ngo-Ngo, and her brother Bong Ngo is called bo-ngo, meaning skull. And the Po girl who married a Que boy gets a name that is unmentionable.

And of course, the Koh family wallows in the Filipino possessive "ko": Mary Koh (my Mary), Peter Koh (my Peter), Richard Koh (My Dick), Theodore T. Koh and Katherine K. Koh become TT Kho and KK Kho respectively.

There are many Filipino words derived from the Chinese. Inchik, for instance, means Uncle, one held in admiration, a sign of respect. Hikao, earring means ear hook. Buaya, Ate (Atsi, elder sister), Ditsi (second sister), Satsi (third) sister, Cuya (A-hya).

Tao means bean. So Tao-yo or toyo means bean sauce. Tao-ho means bean cake. Tao-gue means bean sprouts. Go means cow, To means stomach; Go-to means the stomach of the cow. And so on and so on.

Having migrated here from Indonesia and Malaya, we Filipinos have a lot of common words with our brown brothers. Mukha (face), for instance, and Mata (eyes). Our Tenga (ears) is their Telenga. Our Elong (nose) is their Edong. Our Daan (way) is their Djalan.

But most of our words from Spaniards, who occupied our country for 350 years. Mesa, silla, ventana, mano, puta, derecho, beso, casa, coche, garaje. Chabacano, a corruption of Spanish is a dialect spoken by descendants of Spanish sailors in Cavite and Zamboanga where the Spanish naval

bases use to be located.
January 6, 1995, April 15, 1996, ISYU.

ooooo

CHAPTER 8. Henares and Don Quixote ride again!

In the ancestral home of Diego de Henares, 13th century commander of the King's Archers, and Larry Henares of the Inquirer --- in the Henares Valley in the province of Castile, where flowed the Henares River --- in the little town of Alcala de Henares, locus of the oldest university in Spain --- Miguel Cervantes, along with Shakespeare the greatest of the world's writers, was born.

Spain, once a great colonial power, should have been one of the greatest centers of literature, yet it is not. There have been too many divisions of territory and dialect, it took a long time before the most beautiful of the dialects, that of Castile, became the literary language of Spain.

The Spanish language, by reason of its abounding rimes where all words of feminine gender end with the letter A, and those of the masculine gender with letter O, makes versifying too easy. Poetry and beauty of expression is so easily achieved with the precision and symmetry of the Spanish language that little effort is spent in the choice of expression essential for great literature.

Also, Spain has always been a country where freedom of thought was restricted and the intolerant atmosphere was not conducive to great literature either. For these reasons, Spain has failed to produce a large body of world-class literature.

Yet in Miguel Cervantes of Spain do we find the only writer who can claim to rival Shakespeare. Cervantes was born in 1547, seventeen years before Shakespeare, and died on the day Shakespeare died in 1616. When he was already 58 years old, he wrote one book Don Quixote and 11 years later, six months before he died, he wrote a sequel even better than the first part.

Together the two books of Don Quixote turned out to be a world-class masterpiece which has been translated into more languages than any of Shakespeare's plays, more than any other book other than the Bible. And in the eyes of many, Miguel Cervantes ranks with Shakespeare as the greatest of all writers.

Don Quixote was written to make fun of the outworn practices of chivalry that had become a thoroughly insincere fashion in Spain. As Cervantes went on with his work it grew into a survey of the people who made up the Spanish nation, for that matter the entire human race, as they appeared to a man of humor and broad sympathy, seeing life from many points of view, with a mixture of sadness and amusement. It is a book that one can read many times, always with fresh joy.

THE MAN FROM LA MANCHA is a musical play based on those two books about Miquel Cervantes and Don Quixote, and known for one great song, "The Impossible Dream," probably the favorite of most of the world's leaders, from the Kennedys to Ninoy Aquino to Evelio Javier. Mine too. It definitely is not the favorite of Bernie Villegas, Dick Romulo, Clipper Lorenzo, Christian Monsod and Jimmy Ongpin; theirs is "God Bless America."

For most of us who fight life's lonely battles, those of us who fight for lost causes, which are the only causes really worth fighting and dying for, there is a sense of identification with the hero of Cervantes' story.

The Man from La Mancha, now being performed by Repertory Philippines in the Insular Life Theater Thursday through Sunday up to June 6, tells the story of Cervantes, jailed by the Spanish Inquisition, who recounts for his fellow prisoners, the tale of a slightly deranged old man as a knight errant seeking beauty, virtue, goodness in the midst of corruption, hypocrisy and cynicism.

Miguel Cervantes to the the Jimmy Ongpins of this world:

I have lived for over 40 years and I have seen Life as it is: Pain, Misery, Cruelty beyond belief. I have heard the voices of God's noble creatures moaning from bundles of filth in the streerts. I have seen my comrades fall in battle, or die more slowly by the lash. I held them in my arms at the last moment. These are men who saw Life as it is, and they die despairing, no glory, no brave Last Words, only their eyes filled with confusion, questioning why. I do not think they were questioning why they were dying, but why they had ever lived... Too much sanity may be madness. But maddest of all is to see Life as it is, and not as it should be.

Sung Don Quixote de la Mancha to the Bobbit Sanchezes and Bobby Tañadas of this world:

To dream the impossible dream, to fight the unbeatable foe, to bear with unbearable sorrow, to run where the brave dare not go... To right the unrightable wrong, to love pure and chaste from afar, to try when your arms are too weary, to reach the unreachable star... This is my quest, to follow that star, no matter how hopeless, no matter how far... To fight for the right without question or pause, to be willing to march into hell for a heavenly cause... And I know if I'll only be true to this glorious quest, then my heart will lie peaceful and calm when I'm laid to my rest... And the world could be better for this, that one man scorned and covered with scars, still strove with his last ounce of courage, to reach the unreachable star!

"Have you read Don Quixote?" asked de Guiche of Cyrano de Bergerac.

"I have," answered Cyrano,"and found myself hero."

"Be so good as to read once more the chapter of the windmills. Windmills, remember, if you fight with them, may swing around their huge arms and cast you down into the mud."

And Cyrano answered, "Or up – among the stars!"

.May 21, 1987, Philippine Daily Inquirer

ooooo

End of the Book

9 781986 797627